PERSISTENT YOUNG OFFENDERS

Welfare and Society
Studies in Welfare Policy, Practice and Theory

Series Editors:
Matthew Colton, Kevin Haines, Peter Raynor and Susan Roberts
Swansea University, UK

Welfare and Society is an exciting series from the Department of Applied Social Science at Swansea University, in conjunction with Ashgate, concerned with all aspects of social welfare. The series publishes works of research, theory, history and practice from a wide range of contemporary applied social studies subjects such as Criminal Justice, Child Welfare, Community Care, Race and Ethnicity, Therapeutic and Intervention Techniques, Community Development and Social Policy. The series includes extended research reports of scholarly interest as well as works aimed at both the academic and professional communities.

Also in the series:

Violations of Trust: How Social and Welfare Institutions Fail Children and Young People
Edited by Judith Bessant, Richard Hil and Rob Watts
ISBN 978-0-7546-1872-0 • February 2006

Supervising Offenders in the Community: A History of Probation Theory and Practice
Maurice Vanstone
ISBN 978-0-7546-4190-2 (Hbk) • July 2004
ISBN 978-0-7546-7174-9 (Pbk) • June 2007

Residential Care: Horizons for the New Century
Edited by Hans Göran Eriksson and Torill Tjelflaat
ISBN 978-0-7546-4098-1 • July 2004

Perspectives on Female Sex Offending: A Culture of Denial
Myriam S. Denov
ISBN 978-0-7546-3565-9 • January 2004

Social Justice and the Politics of Community
Christine Everingham
ISBN 978-0-7546-3398-3 • December 2003

Persistent Young Offenders
An Evaluation of Two Projects

DAVID LOBLEY
formerly Lancaster University, UK

DAVID SMITH
Lancaster University, UK

ASHGATE

Published by
Ashgate Publishing Limited
Gower House
Croft Road
Aldershot
Hampshire GU11 3HR
England

Ashgate Publishing Company
Suite 420
101 Cherry Street
Burlington, VT 05401-4405
USA

Ashgate website: http://www.ashgate.com

British Library Cataloguing in Publication Data
Lobley, David
    Persistent young offenders : an evaluation of two projects.
    - (Welfare and society)
    1. CueTen (Program) 2. Freagarrach (Program) 3. Juvenile
    delinquents - Rehabilitation - Scotland 4. Social work with
    juvenile delinquents - Scotland - Evaluation
    I. Title II. Smith, David, 1947 Aug. 2-
    364.6'8'0835'09411

Library of Congress Cataloging-in-Publication Data
Lobley, David.
    Persistent young offenders : an evaluation of two projects / by David Lobley and David Smith.
        p. cm. -- (Welfare and society)
    Includes bibliographical references and index.
    ISBN 978-0-7546-4183-4
    1. Juvenile delinquents--Rehabilitation--Scotland--Case studies. 2. Social work with juvenile delinquents--Scotland--Case studies. 3. Juvenile justice, Administration of--Scotland. I. Smith, David, 1947 Aug. 2- II. Title.

    HV9147.A5L63 2007
    364.3609411--dc22

2007014524

ISBN 978-0-7546-4183-4

Printed and bound in Great Britain by Antony Rowe Ltd, Chippenham, Wiltshire.

Contents

List of Tables

Series Editor's Foreword

The editors of the Welfare and Society series are delighted to publish this exceptionally insightful and illuminating study of two projects in Scotland which were set up to work with young people in trouble with the law. Both evaluations were commissioned by the Scottish Executive. Too often the main result of an evaluation commissioned by an official body is a long report which is read (we hope) by officials, but is not drawn fully to the attention of the academic community. Sometimes this may be the appropriate outcome, but in other cases the research has broader implications which deserve to be more widely read and thought about. This is clearly the case in this study: it not only tells the story of these pioneering projects and the young people who passed through them, but also contributes to our understanding of what is needed to work successfully with young offenders; of how interagency collaboration works, and what happens when it doesn't; of the strengths of Scottish policy and tradition in youth justice, and the opportunities this offers for creative work; and of why evaluative research requires more than a mechanical counting of outputs and outcomes. Such discussions are timely and important when, particularly in England and Wales, the dominant policy themes in youth justice appear to be a politically motivated display of toughness, an increasing reliance on custodial punishment, and an insistence on treating young offenders as criminals first and children second.

This book shows the importance of working with persistent young offenders in a patient, consistent, understanding and resilient way, relying on skilled and experienced workers to apply the evidence-based lessons of 'what works' within the context of a personal relationship and a long-term commitment, rather than the centralised and managerialist approach to the prescription of 'interventions' which has been much criticized in England and Wales. The Scottish policy context, in which services for young people in trouble have emphasized their welfare and their developmental needs rather than concentrating simply on offending and anti-social behaviour, is an important part of the background to these projects, and has been less well studied and understood outside Scotland than it deserves. Finally, students of evaluation methodology will see a good example of methodological triangulation and of the combination of qualitative and quantitative methods, contrasting markedly with the rather one-dimensional approach preferred, and indeed prescribed, by the Home Office[1] (Home Office 2004).

Lancaster University has a distinguished track record in youth justice research, much of it led by David Smith, including the influential 'Lancaster Model' of the 1980s which showed how the use of custodial sentences and residential care for young offenders could be drastically reduced. This book adds to that tradition. We are also pleased to be including another criminological title in the series, to add to

---

1   Home Office (2004) *Home Office and YJB Standards for Impact Studies in Correctional Settings*. London: Home Office Research, Development and Statistics.

the earlier volumes by Kevin Haines on juvenile justice, Myriam Denov on female sex offenders and Maurice Vanstone on the history of the Probation Service. We hope, with the help of the team at Ashgate, to continue to publish high quality studies of this kind.

Peter Raynor
May 2007

Acknowledgements

We owe thanks to many people, some of whom must remain anonymous, for their support for the research presented here. In particular, we want to thank: the staff of the projects, for their hospitality and willingness to be the subjects of research; other members of the staff of Apex Scotland and Barnardo's Scotland; the young people who attended the projects, for the time they gave and the insights they provided, and their parents and other family members; staff of the police and the Reporter's Administration in Fife; and staff in the police, social work, education services and the Reporter's Administration in Clackmannanshire, Falkirk and Stirling, and in the former Central Region. Gary Denman and Tina Stern worked on the Freagarrach evaluation during its early and later stages respectively, and Marc Radley helped with the analysis of data on young offenders in central Scotland; we are grateful for their contributions. In both evaluations we had the support of an Advisory Group in Edinburgh, and benefited from the help and advice of Diane Machin and Joe Curran of the Central Research Unit. We are of course solely responsible for any errors and inadequacies that remain.

Introduction

The core of this book is an account of the evaluation of two projects for persistent juvenile offenders in Scotland, from which, we claim, it is possible to extract messages of general value and continuing importance. One of the projects, Freagarrach, still exists (in late 2006);[1] the other, CueTen, lasted for only three years, from 1995 to 1998, when its funding was stopped. Perhaps the most obvious message of the book is that Freagarrach was a successful project, and that CueTen, while it had its virtues, was much less so; and because we think there is more to be learned from success than from failure (and because it is certainly pleasanter to write and, we hope, read about), we deal with Freagarrach at greater length than with CueTen. We want to be clear from the start, however, that our analysis of the relative failure of CueTen locates its problems in the conception of its purpose, the content of its programme, and the circumstances of its establishment, and not in any deficiencies of its hard-working, thoughtful and helpful staff; and we should also stress that Apex Scotland, which ran the project, is now a very different organisation, has shown itself capable of working successfully with juvenile as well as adult offenders, and has established its credibility in this field (Apex Scotland, 2006).

Important changes, briefly discussed below, took place on the level of Scottish national politics during the period of the evaluation, but a change that occurred earlier also had an impact on the projects, and particularly on Freagarrach, which was conceived and planned as part of an inter-agency strategy for an administrative entity which soon after ceased to exist. At the beginning of 1996 the regional structure of local government in Scotland was largely replaced by a reversion to the older model of smaller unitary authorities. Central Region, in which Freagarrach worked from two sites, Polmont in the south and Alloa in the north, was disaggregated into Clackmannanshire, Falkirk and Stirling. Of these Clackmannanshire, to the north and east of the old region, is the smallest in terms of both area and population; indeed, its population of about 49,000 makes it the smallest local authority in mainland Scotland. The largest of the new authorities in terms of population is Falkirk, with about 144,000 people; it is also the most urban and industrial of the three. Stirling is by far the largest geographically, with a rural area to the west and north stretching into the southern Highlands; most of its population of around 86,000 live in the historic town of Stirling itself. CueTen was located in Glenrothes in Fife partly because local government reorganisation promised to be minimally disruptive there. Fife's population of about 350,000 is larger than the total of the old Central Region, although its area is only about 60 per cent of Stirling's. Glenrothes, the administrative centre, was a post-war New Town whose prosperity, it was hoped,

---

1 It now works from one site, in Stirling, and not from the two it occupied for most of the evaluation period.

would be based on coal mining; unfortunately the mine beside which it was built never proved economically viable.[2]

As in much of Scotland's central belt, there are areas of urban decline and serious deprivation in Fife and the former Central Region, often highly localised and close to sites of historic importance and scenic beauty. Anyone who knows Fife only slightly will tend to associate it with St Andrews, the ancestral home of golf and of Scotland's oldest university, or with attractive fishing villages, rather than with the areas of post-industrial decline, resulting especially from the collapse of coal mining, that are also a feature of the area. Stirling Castle stands on its strategically important rock in the Forth Valley above a town ill-served by urban development and skirted by poor social housing estates, among them one at Bannockburn, the site in 1314 of Scotland's most famous victory in its fight to maintain independence from England. The Ochil Hills that rise steeply from the plain of Clackmannan form a Highland landscape in miniature, but Alloa, Clackmannanshire's largest town, has rates of unemployment and long-term sickness or disability above the Scottish average, and the brewing industry for which it was once known has shrunk to near-invisibility. Falkirk, the site of a battle in the wars of independence in 1297 which tends to receive less local attention because the Scots lost, is less immediately appealing in aesthetic terms than the other areas, but has survived the processes of deindustrialisation relatively well, thanks to the large petro-chemical works at nearby Grangemouth. Overall, while none of these areas has anything like the extent of deprivation found in parts of Glasgow, they are all characterised by social and economic divisions which mean that attractive and prosperous urban districts often exist next to neighbourhoods marked by social, environmental and economic damage.

Changes in Politics and Policy

The projects were evaluated over the period 1995–2001, thus spanning a time of important constitutional change in Scotland, which culminated in the first elections to the Scottish Parliament in May 1999. This devolution of important areas of political power has led to changes in policy on young offenders, as in other spheres of social and criminal justice policy, and the policy environment of 2006 differs from that in which the projects were established. The election of 1999, using a system of proportional representation, led to control of the Scottish Executive by a Labour-Liberal Democrat coalition, with the Scottish National Party (SNP) the largest party in opposition; the result of the 2003 election was the same, though the SNP strengthened its position, mainly at Labour's expense. The pre-devolution system of juvenile justice in Scotland, established by the Social Work (Scotland) Act of 1968, was distinctive in being a 'full-fledged, welfare-oriented system' (Bottoms, 2002: 254), and by the time Bottoms was writing was a 'relatively rare surviving example' of such a system among western nations. It had long attracted international attention for the priority it gave to the best interests of children, its relative indifference to

---

2   All the information about the areas in which the projects were located comes from the 2001 census and related (and more recent) material on associated websites. See http://www. scrol.gov.uk/scrol/common/home.jsp and the relevant local government sites.

whether children in trouble were also offenders, and its lack of provision of punitive measures (Lockyer and Stone, 1998); and given its status as a distinctively Scottish achievement, it might have been (and was) hoped that it would remain safe after devolution (Smith, 2000). Up to a point, this has been the case, though the exclusive focus on the child's welfare has been modified by a provision that the system may also take the public interest into account (Doob and Tonry, 2004); but it is also the case that youth offending has become a political issue since the creation of the Scottish parliament in a way that it was not before devolution.

There were early signs that the Scottish Executive would indeed not only maintain the Children's Hearings System (CHS) but might extend its scope to include 16–17 year-olds as well as children under 16. This was the proposal of the report of an Advisory Group on Youth Crime set up shortly after the 1999 election (Scottish Executive, 2000), and it was largely accepted by the Executive; but the report recognised that if this was to be achieved it would require a substantial injection of new resources into the CHS. A subsequent report (Audit Scotland, 2002) had, according to Whyte (2003: 80), more political impact, and 'fuelled an ongoing political debate…The political consensus of 2000 proved short-lived, and the politicisation of youth justice in Scotland dominated the run up' to the 2003 election. By the summer of 2002 Scottish Ministers were talking both about putting more resources into the CHS to fast-track persistent offenders and about establishing a pilot youth court for 16–17-year-old persistent offenders, an option specifically rejected three years before (Smith, 2003). Some of the policy complexity, or perhaps confusion, and the political capital the SNP and Conservatives tried to make from it, is illustrated in the following exchange from the Official *Record* of the Scottish Parliament for 13 June 2002 (at http://www.scottish.parliament.uk/business/officialReports/meetingsParliament/or-02/sor0613-02.htm#Col12706); the excerpt may also shed light on the style with which Members of the Scottish Parliament conduct their business:

The First Minister (Mr Jack McConnell): I take this opportunity to wish Mr Swinney [MSP for North Tayside, and at the time leader of the SNP] a happy birthday – I believe it is his birthday today.

Members: Aw.

The Presiding Officer (Sir David Steel): No singing, please…

Mr Swinney: I thank the First Minister for the birthday greetings. I am sorry to tell him that today is not my birthday… My advice to the First Minister is not to believe the rubbish that he reads in the newspapers. I have a quote for the First Minister: 'the juvenile courts system in England is a disaster. Even with fast tracking, it is an absolute disaster, and they look with considerable envy at the hearings system, even with its flaws. So, to suggest that courts are going to be the solution is not the answer'. Is that the view of the Government?

The First Minister: It is wrong of Mr Swinney to take out of context a remark that was made this morning… It is quite clear that the development of youth courts in Scotland is an option that we should look at to deal with the serious problems of young offenders in Scotland...

Mr Swinney: ...We have had strategy after ministerial review after strategy after working group, but the problem of youth crime has not gone away. When will the First Minister speak clearly on youth crime and when will his ministers follow his direction? ... When will the First Minister start to listen to the people of Scotland and deliver real action on youth crime?

The First Minister: ...There is a problem in our youth justice system in the way in which it addresses the middle teenage years. The children's hearings system is not coping and the adult courts are turning young offenders into permanent adult offenders. That problem needs to be tackled...

David McLetchie (Lothians) (Con): ... Assault, robbery, breach of the peace, vandalism and more are referred to the children's hearings system under the present system, which the First Minister wants to extend. The First Minister is in complete and utter disarray on the issue and is at odds with his ministers. When Richard Simpson said this morning that the First Minister's youth courts idea would be a disaster, was he speaking for the Executive or for himself? Are the youth courts still on the agenda or are they dead in the water? ...

The First Minister: ...We need to consider options such as youth courts precisely because of the important issue that Mr McLetchie identified – the number of youngsters in their mid-teenage years who commit serious offences and the lack of public confidence in the ability of the children's hearings system to deal with them...

Roseanna Cunningham (Perth) (SNP): The First Minister is in trouble.... The First Minister should just sit down...

The First Minister: The SNP is heating up in its cauldron today. The cauldron is getting a bit hot before the weekend. At least there is a full turnout today. [Interruption.]

The Executive did continue to consider the youth court option, and the first pilot court was established in Hamilton in June 2003, followed just over a year later by a second in Airdrie – both towns in Scotland's central belt (Piacentini and Walters, 2006). While commentators concerned with the welfare of juvenile offenders, and with the maintenance of the distinctively Scottish approach to youth justice, might console themselves with the thought that the youth courts were at least diverting young offenders from the adult system, Piacentini and Walters argue that it is not clear that this was actually what the pilot courts did. They see the youth court as 'simply an adult court setting masquerading as a fast-track youth process' (2006, 55). This aspect of it was, however, found to be successful in bringing cases to a swift conclusion and dealing more efficiently with breaches of orders (Popham et al, 2005), which enabled the Executive to announce in November 2006 that in view of the 'broadly positive' findings of the evaluation of the pilots funding would be made available for up to three further youth courts (Scottish Executive press release at http://www.scotland.gov.uk/News/Releases/2006/11/24101019). While the tone of the press release is modest rather than triumphant, and at the time the number and location of the new courts had not been finally decided, there is no doubt that the suggestion that the pilots had been successful enough for the idea to be extended elsewhere represents a move away from the principles of the CHS, and another stage in what McAra (2006: 142) calls the 'detartanisation' of youth justice in Scotland. After a long period of notable stability, during which it enjoyed the strong support of those who served it (Kelly, 1996a), and threats to it (mostly from the Conservative Government in London) were in general successfully repulsed (Lockyer and Stone, 1998), the CHS has undergone more critical scrutiny and more erosion of its central principles in the seven years since devolution than in the almost 30 years of its pre-devolution existence.

As McAra (2006) argues, Scottish ministers have adopted much of the 'New Labour' agenda on youth crime and justice, which for all its ambiguities includes an acceptance that punishment is a legitimate aim of the system, and stresses the centrality of public protection and risk management. While typically implemented a few years later than in England and Wales, Anti-Social Behaviour Orders, electronic monitoring, curfews and Parenting Orders are now part of the legal apparatus of the youth justice system in Scotland. Organisational arrangements have also come to resemble those of England and Wales, with the creation of inter-agency youth justice teams that mirror the Youth Offending Teams established a few years earlier. McAra (2006:142) sees the philosophy that underpinned the CHS from its inception as under threat from new measures 'which have begun to place deeds rather than needs at the forefront of decision-making processes'. But this is not to say that the youth justice system in Scotland has entirely abandoned its historic emphasis on the welfare of children or become indistinguishable in its aims and priorities from the system south of the border. For example, there has been nothing comparable with the rebranding of the probation service in England and Wales as something other than a social work agency (Smith, 2005), and even in the youth court setting official policy in Scotland still assumes that the appropriate services will come from social workers. In relation to the CHS, a press release of 19 December 2006 quotes the Education Minister Hugh Henry as saying, in introducing a consultation on the draft Children's Services (Scotland) Bill:

> We know that the children's hearing system has dealt very effectively with both the needs and deeds of young people in Scotland for the past 30 years. Our consultation confirmed the system works and is respected. But reform is needed to cope with the challenges of children's lives in the 21st century. The current level of referrals is not sustainable and too many children are going through the system as a way of accessing support and services. This slows everything down (at http://www.scotland.gov.uk/News/Releases/2006/12/19114616).

Typically, in Scotland new measures are introduced more slowly and tentatively than in England and Wales, and after processes of consultation that allow for the expression of qualifications and dissent. Policy implementation is less *dirigiste* and imperative than south of the border, no doubt because Scotland is relatively a small society and members of its élites are highly interconnected. In the case of the youth courts, 18 months elapsed between the reporting of positive results from their evaluation and the cautious suggestion of their expansion. The Executive has been at least equally cautious in its approach to reform of the CHS, even though, as hinted by Hugh Henry, it might be difficult to argue that a system established in 1971 (and based on a report from 1964) needed no reform at all.

The case of the Freagarrach Project serves as an illustration of the ambiguities of Scottish youth justice policy. As we will show, it works on a basis of voluntary attendance and with no deterrent sanctions for failure to attend it, a model which was and is literally inconceivable south of the border. Its survival testifies to a continuing commitment to a non-punitive, welfare orientation; and the fact that it remains the only project of its kind testifies to the political difficulty of celebrating it as a model for practice with young offenders in Scotland. Freagarrach stands alone despite general recognition of its success: the report from Audit Scotland (2002), parts of which, as noted above, were used in the process of politicisation of youth justice, argued that

> a 10% reduction in the total costs of secure care, residential care and YOIs [Young Offender Institutions] would release £6 million. This would fund 10 services similar to Freagarrach (widely recognised as an effective services [sic] for persistent offenders), catering for around 1000 children each year, shifting funds from more expensive options into intensive community support at an earlier stage, and thereby increasing the overall effectiveness of the system (Audit Scotland, 2002: 71).

The report criticised local authorities for being slow to follow Freagarrach's example, but, as we will explain, Freagarrach only came into being because of a central government initiative, and support for it from within its own local authorities came into question during the period of our evaluation. Neither locally nor nationally are Scottish politics immune to the appeal of the penal populism that has been so influential on criminal justice policy south of the border (for example Goldson and Muncie, 2006).

The Structure of the Book

Chapter 1 describes and analyses the establishment of Freagarrach and CueTen. It notes the policy context which enabled them to come into existence, and the important differences in the local circumstances in which they began their work, Freagarrach being seen as an organic development of an existing local strategy, CueTen as a new and largely unheralded stranger whose arrival was met with suspicion in some quarters. Chapter 2 describes the work of CueTen, in theory and practice, showing that the innovative aims and methods which had been a main part of its appeal to the Scottish Office were difficult to implement in practice. Chapter 3 similarly describes the work of Freagarrach, showing how the project benefited from its embeddedness in a range of local services and from high-level support in local agencies. It discusses the day to day work of the project staff, and suggests that while their approach was certainly in line with the best available evidence about 'what works' it was also crucially informed by relationships with the young people that conveyed care and respect as well as setting firm limits on what counted as acceptable behaviour.

Chapter 4 presents the characteristics of the young people who attended the projects. Both CueTen and Freagarrach largely succeeded in working with their intended target groups of the most persistent juvenile offenders in their areas. CueTen worked mainly with 15 year-olds, Freagarrach with a wider age range, but mainly from 14 to 16. Very few were attending school in any meaningful sense. As with all populations of known persistent offenders, the great majority were male, and many had experienced deprivation, loss and abuse in their family lives, and were enmeshed in subcultures of delinquency and substance misuse. Chapter 5 discusses how the projects were perceived by the young people who attended them, and by social workers and other staff in the juvenile justice system. While the young people and (when we could obtain their views) their relatives spoke positively about their experience of the projects, the chapter stresses the importance of the organisational context in which they worked, and the continuing difficulties faced by CueTen as a result of the circumstances of the project's establishment.

Chapter 6 turns to the question of the projects' effectiveness, defined primarily as their impact on the young people's rate and seriousness of offending, but also in terms of effects on the use of secure residential care and custody. It was rare for young people who attended the projects to stop offending entirely (insofar as this can be known from data sources of variable quality), but this is not surprising given the volume and intensity of their offending before they started at the projects. Freagarrach had substantially more impact on reoffending than CueTen, and correspondingly more influence in reducing the demand for care or custody. An attempt is made to estimate the number and nature of the offences that may have been prevented by the projects' work, and their effect in reducing the number and length of long-term criminal careers. Chapter 7 examines the costs of the projects and sets these against the benefits they produced in reduced rates of offending and reduced demand for other resources. Using a relatively conservative estimate of the costs of offending, it argues that Freagarrach, while at first glance an expensive project, probably prevented enough offending in the short and longer terms to be judged highly cost-effective. Chapter 8 draws together themes from the earlier chapters to provide an overall evaluation of the two projects, and argues that the success of Freagarrach also counts as a success for the principles of welfare and voluntarism that have always underpinned the Children's Hearings System – perhaps the book's single most important message.

Chapter 1

The Establishment of the Projects

The Legislative Context

By virtue of the 1968 Social Work (Scotland) Act, Scotland acquired a distinctive system for dealing with juvenile offenders, and one that entailed a radical commitment to children's needs rather to their formal legal rights. This is the Children's Hearings System (CHS), which replaced juvenile courts in 1971, and represents a thorough-going commitment to the primacy of welfare rather than justice in responding to offending by juveniles. The CHS is an expression of the philosophy set out in the report of the Kilbrandon Committee (Scottish Home and Health Department, 1964): that, in general, criminal courts do not provide an appropriate setting for dealing with young offenders, because their work is based on the assumption of a degree of personal responsibility which unrealistically ignores the characteristics of children and young people that differentiate them from adults. Instead, the Kilbrandon Committee recommended that – with the exception of the most serious offences – offending by children and young people up to the age of 16 should be regarded as just one of a range of problems that might require official intervention, and should be dealt with by a tribunal that was explicitly not a criminal court. Thus, the CHS is inherently a system of diversion from criminal justice processes (Whyte, 2000), and offending is just one of a number of 'grounds of referral' which can bring children to the attention of the Reporter to the CHS, who will then decide what, if any, action is required.

In cases where the Reporter decides that the matter requires that the child or young person ('child' will be used in the following discussion for the sake of simplicity) be referred to a Children's Panel, rather than being dealt with informally, the experience of the hearing is, by design, very different from the experience of appearing in a criminal court. The panel members are lay people, drawn from the local community, and they have no power to decide issues of guilt and innocence; if the child does not accept the ground of referral, the case may be sent to a Sheriff Court, which, if it finds that there is sufficient evidence, will normally send it back to the CHS for a decision. The task of the Panel members is to reach a decision based on consideration of the best interests of the child. They are there to resolve difficulties, not to blame or punish. The style of Hearings is meant to be open and informal, so as to provide maximum opportunities for the active involvement of children and their carers in reaching an agreed solution. It is non-adversarial, since the Hearing will not take place unless all present agree on the basic facts, and the child has no right to legal representation, although a lawyer may attend as a friend or supporter. While the Panel has no power to impose any punitive sentence, it does have the power to order 'compulsory measures of care', which can include supervision with a residential requirement, if it believes that these are the best means of promoting the child's welfare. No formal punitive sanctions are available should the child fail to comply with the requirements of supervision; for example, the CueTen project worked with young people who had been required by a Hearing to attend its programme, but no penalty existed for failure to turn up, or to complete the programme. The ideal of the CHS is that decisions should be consensual, reflecting the outcome of a discussion in which all are concerned to serve the best interests of the child.

The CHS, with its commitment to a process of decision-making which is non-adversarial and specifically intended as a diversion from criminal justice processes, is exceptional among juvenile justice systems. Lockyer and Stone (1998: 256) argue that the international discourse of children's rights, expressed in such United Nations statements as the Beijing Rules (1985), the Riyadh Guidelines (1990) and the Havana Rules (1990), tends to assume that children who offend will be dealt with by a body with the characteristics of a court, on the grounds that this is the only means of safeguarding their rights. According to Fox (1991), the British representatives at the Geneva meeting which agreed the UN Convention on the Rights of the Child in 1989 were unaware of how far the CHS departed from this model, particularly in its bar on legal representation. In ratifying the Convention, the British government entered the reservation that it would maintain the CHS in its existing form, which had proved effective over the years. Thus, at the time of the establishment of the projects discussed in this book Scotland had, as it continues to have, a system for dealing with children in trouble which is something of an anomaly by international standards, but which has – in general and despite some tinkering – continued to be supported in Scotland both by politicians and by those who work within the system (Lockyer and Stone, 1998; Scottish Executive, 2000). This is not to say that the system is viewed as perfect or incapable of improvement; indeed, it was dissatisfaction with aspects of its operation that gave rise to the initiatives that made the Freagarrach and CueTen projects possible.

The Policy Context

In the early 1990s, a source of frustration for policy-makers and juvenile justice practitioners was the limited range of resources available for juveniles repeatedly referred to the CHS on grounds of offending. According to civil servants interviewed in the course of our work, the Scottish Office at that time received regular complaints from practitioners about the inadequacy of resources available to deal effectively with such persistent offenders, who, while relatively few in number, were responsible for a high proportion of juvenile crime. While there was then less pressure in Scotland than south of the border for overtly punitive measures (McIvor, 1994), because of the continued general acceptance of the principles of care built into the CHS (Kelly, 1996a), the Scottish Office wished to take these complaints seriously, and was interested in developing strategies which would provide the Children's Hearings with additional options for disposal, and if possible begin to provide answers to the longer-term problems underlying persistent juvenile offending.

The Social Work Services Group and the Crime Prevention Unit within the Scottish Office had mutual interests in finding constructive solutions, and established a working alliance aimed at a long-term reduction in crime and its associated social problems. A central problem was that the Children's Panels had few middle-range alternatives at their disposal between the poles of residential care and home supervision, 'which in reality', according to one interviewee, 'was one hour a week with a social worker' (if that, one might add). Discussions in the Scottish Office led to agreement that some intermediate options were required, particularly for 14–15 year-olds, the age group in which persistent offending seemed to be concentrated. If successful, these new measures should therefore have a medium-term crime reduction effect, in line with an emerging interest in social (offender-focused) crime prevention. The concept of the 'persistent juvenile offender' was central to these discussions, and lengthy debates apparently took place on how to define frequency or persistence of offending. While no single definition emerged, it was agreed that funding of new initiatives would be confined to projects which made a public commitment to working specifically with persistent offenders. It was also agreed that the strategy should be one which maintained the traditional welfare orientation of the CHS, and that projects should be encouraged to address and try to influence offending behaviour within a framework that should include issues such as individual motivation and the stimulation of new interests and potentials, rather than concentrating solely on the act of offending itself.

The hope was that this approach would be effective in dealing with the immediate problem of persistent offending, and also produce guidance on the most promising longer-term strategy. One interviewee, who had been involved in these early discussions, explained:

> we all have to pursue a purposeful quest to get answers to such long-term difficult problems. We don't just want a scheme to cope with today's joyriders, but one that can cope with the more sophisticated thieves of tomorrow.

The aim was, then, to encourage a broad, 'programme-driven' strategic approach, rather than merely a number of discrete short-term projects (King, 1988). The main outcome of these deliberations that is relevant here was the announcement by the then Minister of State, Lord Fraser, at the Scottish Police Federation's annual conference in 1994, of his intention

> to promote a major new community based initiative designed to intervene in the behaviour of persistent young offenders who account for a disproportionate number of crimes and offences (Scottish Office, 1994).

The immediate origins of both the Freagarrach and the CueTen projects lay in this announcement, which took up a theme from the 1993 White Paper, *Scotland's Children*:

> Effective supervision in the community is also needed for those whose persistent offending makes them a nuisance to the neighbourhoods in which they live or whose disturbed behaviour makes them a serious risk to themselves and others. More intensive supervision

arrangements are required for a small number of young people and these arrangements should be developed from existing intermediate treatment and groupwork projects and the establishment of new ones so that the resource is available at least in each major urban area (Scottish Office, 1993, para. 7.23).

The Scottish Office invited six voluntary child care organisations to submit proposals for pilot projects, and copies of the invitation were sent to the Chief Executives of the Regional and Islands Councils and to Directors of Social Work. It was made clear in the specification that 'the schemes proposed will be required to attract the support and collaboration of Social Work Directors and indeed local children's panels — as well as the police and the education service' (Scottish Office, 1994), and that 'proposals should therefore be presented in conjunction with the appropriate local authorities'. Grants totalling about £200,000 per annum for a period of five years were to be made available, with the suggestion that this could be 'augmented' in cash or in kind by the local authorities and/or the voluntary organisations. The specification envisaged that projects would be located in two areas, to enable comparisons that would inform the development of best practice for possible replication in other parts of Scotland. The aim of the projects should be to reduce the demand for secure residential care, through the development of innovative practice with persistent juvenile offenders.

The Origins of Freagarrach

In the event, only one project was initially funded, in what was then Central Region, the area now covered by Clackmannanshire, Falkirk and Stirling. This was what was to become Freagarrach. Staff in the Scottish Office interviewed near the start of the evaluation were in no doubt that the crucial factors in the success of the bid were the existence of a coherent inter-agency strategy and the credibility that the voluntary organisation concerned, Barnardo's Scotland, had established with the relevant agencies: 'We were tremendously impressed by the inter-agency reaction…Impressed by Bill Wilson [Chief Constable] and his commitment to TRACE'. (TRACE, the importance of which is discussed below, was the computerised information system on juvenile offenders used by Central Scotland Police.) Furthermore, 'they [Barnardo's] had also reached over to the Children's Panel and got the Reporter's confidence.' Barnardo's impressed the Scottish Office officials as 'determined catalysts' already well established in the region as providers of special education and intermediate treatment services, but it was the inter-agency dimension of the proposal, which was also strongly stressed in the presentation at the Scottish Office, that was most important to its success.

Barnardo's had to work fast in preparing the proposal, since the Scottish Office's schedule allowed for only three months between the issue of the outline specification and the presentation of the tender in July 1994. In order to make the deadline Barnardo's had to bypass its own committee structure, through which approval for such a major development would normally be obtained. Its organisation proved flexible enough to allow for executive approval, which was later ratified by the relevant committees. Barnardo's staff were, however, somewhat uneasy about the speed of the process, and about its competitive nature, to which they were unused.

There was some concern that a partnership with one authority might offend others, and alienate them from Barnardo's, and some anxiety about the effect the competition might have on relations among the voluntary organisations themselves.

As well as this organisational flexibility, Barnardo's was able to demonstrate in its proposal first-hand knowledge that a coherent inter-agency strategy was already in place, and how the proposed project would fit into it. The proposal was convincing in giving evidence of thorough knowledge of the regional strategy on young people and of Barnardo's credibility with the key agencies. The presence of existing good relationships between Barnardo's and statutory agencies in Central Region was modestly described by a senior manager as 'a happy coincidence', but it was a coincidence which strengthened the proposal enormously by allowing what became the Freagarrach project to be presented as a logical extension of the existing range of services. TRACE data were used to show the extent of the problem of persistent offending by young people in Central Region (according to a well-defined criterion of persistence), and therefore to establish an empirical case for a specialist project (58 young people were identified as having had five or more 'episodes of offending' in the previous year). The proposal would have been very different without its practical evidence of support at chief officer level in the key agencies, and it seems likely that this was what crucially distinguished it from the other bids considered.

While the tight time scale for tendering presented some problems for Barnardo's, it may in practice have been helpful. Many people have found that an imminent deadline concentrates the mind; in this case, the short time available may also have increased awareness of the strength of the existing partnership and of the value and accessibility of the TRACE data. Insofar as what is at issue here is a 'happy coincidence', there may be an implication that future invitations to tender for similar projects should allow a longer preparation period, to enable, in particular, a thorough empirical demonstration of need. On the other hand, it could be argued that a soundly-based inter-agency strategy should include ready access to relevant data, and that a longer preparation period could encourage proposals in which 'partnerships' were established for purely presentational purposes, with no substantial basis in practice (see Crawford, 1997).

The Scottish Office publicly announced the award of the tender for the development project to Barnardo's, in association with Central Region, at the end of August 1994. Interviews for the post of Project Leader were held in November. The person appointed, Kelly Bayes, had worked in Central Region for many years, and was well known to staff in the relevant agencies and fully aware of the inter-agency strategy and the potential of the TRACE system. Her official starting date in her new post was 20 February 1995, but she was able to take part in preparatory work on the project before her formal appointment. She was joined shortly afterwards by a Project Administrator. Job descriptions for all the remaining posts were drawn up in January 1995, and interviews were arranged for the following two months. The project, not yet named, was to operate from two centres, one in the south (in Polmont, near Falkirk) and one in the north (in the event, in Alloa) of the Region. Each centre was to be run by a senior social worker and three project workers, with support staff, in line with the original proposal. The two senior posts were filled towards the end of March, both those appointed coming from jobs in Central Region Social

Work Department that involved work with young people. In April and May three project workers were appointed by Barnardo's, all with qualifications in Community Education. Central Region was to second three workers to the project; the first two, both with experience in residential child care, started work in April, and the third, who completed the staff team, in October.

Scottish Office staff interviewed about the establishment of the project reported that they had had some anxieties in early 1995 about apparent delays in getting it 'up and running'. The main delay was over finding suitable premises for the project's northern site; the Regional Council could not identify a suitable building, as had originally been hoped, and Barnardo's Property Services and the Project Director herself began to look for premises in Alloa. These were finally identified in May; builders began work in early July; and project staff were able to move in on 1 September. This undoubtedly represented a slippage from the original timetable, but by this time the project was well established at the other site in Polmont, to which Barnardo's had gained access in February. Building work was not finally completed until the beginning of May, but office accommodation and a meeting room had been available from the end of March. 'Minor hiccups' mentioned by the Project Director (Bayes, 1996) were interference on telephone lines, a tendency for mail to be delivered in error to the nearby Polmont Young Offenders Institution, and visits to the project by a mouse or mice.

Much of the Project Director's work in the first months of her appointment was concerned with discussing means of ensuring that the project had access to relevant information and educational resources. It was arranged that she should have direct access to TRACE through a terminal in the project building and that seven places in Special Education Units should be set aside specifically for young people attending the project and excluded from, or for other reasons unable to attend, mainstream school. She also arranged meetings with Children's Panel members, Victim Support groups, Intermediate Treatment projects, SACRO (the Scottish Association for the Care and Resettlement of Offenders), and social work teams, and responded to requests to provide training and contribute to conferences. She began to set up systems for data collection and storage which, as well as meeting the project's own information needs, would be useful for external evaluation. With other Barnardo's staff, she became a member of the Central Region inter-agency Young Offenders Strategy Implementation Group, which met for the first time in March 1995.

When other members of the project team were appointed, the Project Director worked with them to develop referral procedures, guidelines on policy and practice, and information for young people, their parents and social workers. These were produced in May 1995. The information for children and their parents included clear statements about what was expected from them as well as what they could expect from the project. This was particularly important as the team was agreed that young people should attend the project voluntarily, on a basis of invitation and acceptance, although as persistent offenders they would usually already be subject to statutory supervision. The project's commitment to an open access policy on client records was stressed, and its policy on child protection issues was explained. The written material was extended in September, when a booklet on admissions criteria was sent to all relevant agencies, and the project staff made continuing efforts to keep social workers informed of developments, by visiting social work and criminal justice teams and inviting social workers to the open days held at both the project sites. Bayes (1996: 4) reported that the project had the capacity to work with 20 young people at any one time, and anticipated that over a year it would work with about 40 (on the assumption that the average length of an individual programme would be about six months).

The emphasis on voluntary attendance (albeit against the background of a statutory order) might have surprised Lord Fraser, who had stressed in his speech that: 'The new programmes… are not a soft option; they will be intensive, requiring compulsory attendance which will include evenings and weekends where necessary'. Although it is not unusual for politicians to use a language which practitioners might find unfamiliar when describing social work programmes, other statements from around the same time also implied that the project would provide a direct service to the Children's Hearings, with the implication that attendance would be a condition of supervision. It is less clear that this was ever how Barnardo's and its Central Region partners understood the project's purposes: the successful proposal assumed that all young people referred would be subject to statutory supervision, and did envisage referrals from the Reporter, through a 'fast-track' process made possible by access to TRACE, but it also predicted a high demand for the project from social work teams. It was also envisaged by the Director of Social Work that the project would take referrals of young people returning home from residential care outwith Central Region (Bayes, 1996). In the event, the main route to attendance at the project was, from the outset, via a referral (sometimes prompted by the Project Director) from a social worker, and the young people's attendance was, with the exception of a few whose attendance was required by a Probation Order, voluntary, against the background of a statutory order. The first young offender to be accepted by the project began to attend in early June of 1995.

It was about this time (the exact moment is unclear) that the project acquired a name, apparently after much debate. 'Freagarrach' is a Scots Gaelic adjective defined by MacAlpine and Mackenzie (1973) as 'answering, answerable, suitable, fitting'. There may be advantages in a name which, at least to the great majority of young people attending the project, will be empty of emotional resonances, except those associated with a vague feeling that it is probably from the Gaelic. For anyone who did know the meaning of the word, its ambiguity could usefully convey both that the project aimed to provide a suitable service for the young people who attended it and that they were themselves answerable for the way in which they responded to the help offered.

The Origins of CueTen

The parent organisation of the CueTen project, Apex Scotland, was involved in one of the unsuccessful bids for funding under the initiative which led to the establishment of Freagarrach. Apex Scotland began work in 1987, with the aim of improving the chances in the labour market of people with a criminal record, and in the belief that employment should promote desistance from offending; its sister organisation south of the border was well established (see Soothill (1974) for an account of its early work). Initially concerned with adults, the new organisation quickly became aware that employment or the lack of it was also an issue for young offenders, and in 1988 commissioned a study to examine what Apex could do to increase the employment opportunities open to them. The subsequent report (Hurley, 1989) suggested that there was general support among staff of relevant agencies for the principle that there should be a comprehensive inter-agency strategy for those excluded for whatever reason from mainstream education and training. Hurley also found that employers were more willing to help the younger age group, regarding them as more capable of reform, as presenting fewer risks, and perhaps as more deserving of support than adult offenders. The report also suggested that although 'Apex does not have a major role to play at this stage' in working with 'children under supervision from a Children's Hearing', it might become involved in

> liaising with the Children's Panel, Careers, Social Work, and Education departments on the availability and nature of employment and training opportunities for those about to become sixteen, in order to ensure that these young people are fully alerted to such opportunities (Hurley, 1989: 44).

Although the original bid in which it was a partner was unsuccessful, Apex's focus on employment appealed to the Scottish Office officials who judged the bids, and they were also impressed by what they saw as Apex's style, which consciously emphasised a practical rather than cerebral approach. As a result, and to her surprise, the then Director of Apex Scotland, Jeane Freeman, was invited to a meeting at the Scottish Office in January 1995 'to talk about work with young people'. Freeman, who was to become a special adviser to Scotland's First Minister, Jack McConnell, from 2001 to 2005, was evidently once again persuasive, and was invited to submit a proposal for another pilot project. It was to have a distinctive focus on employment, rather than being another social work project, and the Scottish Office hoped that the use of the world of (prospective) work as a medium for engaging the most persistent young offenders would help to define a new and effective approach to juvenile delinquency. In this sense the proposed project was outside the then emerging orthodoxy about 'what works' with offenders (McIvor, 1990; McGuire, 1995), but there were good reasons to believe that Apex's approach could have an impact on the risk of reoffending. Criminological control theory predicts that positive attitudes to education and training will be associated with a reduced risk of delinquency among young people, and the fact of having a job should increase the 'stake in conformity' which means that one has something to lose by offending (Braithwaite, 1989). The meta-analysis of evaluative research by Lipsey (1995) provides empirical support for this prediction, suggesting that employment-based programmes for juvenile offenders show good results compared with other approaches (though this is not true of programmes based solely on vocationally-oriented counselling). There is also evidence that unemployment is associated with an increased rate of offending, both in the lives of individuals (Farrington et al., 1986) and, in respect of recorded property crime, at the level of the national economy (Field, 1990). Sampson and Laub (1993), in their re-working of the Gluecks' data on delinquency, concluded that job stability was the key variable in building the 'social capital' which reduced the risk of an adult criminal career. On a more cautious note, Downes (1993) discusses American evidence which suggests that, while for young offenders (in their mid to late teens) any job is protective against conviction, for young adults (in their late teens to early twenties) the protective effect is only found if the job is a reasonably good one (in terms of wages, security and prospects).

Apex Scotland moved quickly, since the perception in the Scottish Office perception that this was an organisation committed to action rather than words was also Apex's perception of itself, and a proposal reached the Scottish Office in March 1995. This envisaged a project working on two sites, preferably in 'urban and non-urban settings', to allow for the programme's 'applicability and value to be as widely tested as possible within the constraints of a pilot', and providing a service for 48 young offenders over a year. Attendance at the project would be a condition of a Supervision Requirement from the Children's Hearing, and the first 'programme objective' was 'to increase the supervision options available to the Children's Hearing system for use with those young people persistently appearing before Panels on offence grounds'. This statutory basis for the project was clearly in line with the original thinking behind Lord Fraser's announcement of a new initiative on persistent young offenders; but it would have been Apex's preference in any case, on the grounds that this would increase the confidence of Panel members in the project.

The Scottish Office, however, envisaged a project operating from a single site, and Apex revised its proposal accordingly, in consultation with Scottish Office staff. The proposal that was eventually accepted by the Scottish Office, which agreed in July 1995 to fund it for three years, was for a project based in Glenrothes, but serving the whole of Fife, which would work with 32 14–16 year-olds a year. Fife was an attractive location for Apex because it already had an established presence there, and premises for the project were available (unit Q 10 on an industrial estate – hence CueTen); it was also hoped that Fife would suffer relatively little from the local government reorganisation of April 1996. The question of whether Fife had a large enough population to produce the envisaged number of persistent juvenile offenders was not closely considered.

In the summer of 1995 Apex staff worked with members of the Social Work Department in Fife, whose Director was a strong supporter of the project, to refine and agree the criteria for referral to the project. Both parties were content for these to remain relatively broad, in order to allow room for flexibility and professional judgement, rather than trying to define persistence very specifically (a contrast with the line taken by Freagarrach and Central Region). The criteria that were agreed, and appeared in Apex's publicity material for the project, were as follows. The project would consider referrals of young people aged 14–16 'for whom statutory measures have not proved satisfactory or appropriate', and who had appeared before a Children's Hearing on grounds of persistent or escalating offending, were resident in Fife, were at risk of custody or residential care, and had had the CueTen programme explained to them and agreed to meet its requirements.

Apex was also active in recruiting staff for the six posts required for the project. The successful applicants started work on 25 September 1995. In line with Apex's general policy of recognising the relevance of a wide range of skills and experience, the backgrounds of the staff were mixed. None was a social worker, another deliberate feature of Apex's staffing policies: its view was that there was no need to replicate skills that were available elsewhere, and that it could and should offer something distinctive. Only the person appointed to the team leader's post was already working for Apex; she had experience of working with older teenagers, which had led her to feel that the same methods could be successfully applied to a younger age group. Of the others, one was a qualified teacher who wanted to change tack, and was able to persuade Apex that her style was sufficiently open and participative for the project; one had recently obtained a qualification in community education as a mature student, and had considerable experience as a volunteer; one was an ex-farmer who had more recently worked in youth training in agriculture; one had a background in training in the commercial sector; and one was a general administrator. Apex was seeking to appoint a team in which varied skills and aptitudes would complement each other, but all the staff needed to show that they could be authoritative when necessary, as well as work flexibly as part of a team.

The staff began to work informally with a few young people towards the end of 1995, and the first formal programme started in January 1996, attended by ten young people. The programme, as set out in the proposal for the Scottish Office, was to last for 26 weeks, organised in three blocks. The first block, of 13 weeks, consisted of group work with a focus on employment-related attitudes and behaviour, and cognitive and negotiating skills. It included an introduction to vocational training and educational choices, and work on skills and knowledge relevant to getting and keeping a job. The second block, of seven weeks, emphasised individual counselling rather than group work, though group experiences would continue in the form of sports and adventure activities, creative arts, and the development of computing and IT skills. Counselling was to focus on plans for employment or the achievement of related goals through vocational training and college-based work, with a return to mainstream schooling if appropriate. The final block of six weeks was to focus on putting plans into action, identifying key tasks for their implementation and barriers to their achievement, and planning the support the young people would need after leaving the project. In practice the distinction between the second and third blocks quickly became blurred, and it makes more sense to treat the programme as one of 26 weeks divided into two halves, the first requiring near full-time attendance at the project, the second involving part-time attendance and a mix of work placements and college classes (or phased return to school). It was thus an ambitious programme in terms both of its aims and of the expectations it placed on the young people; and, since the groups were closed, with a fixed membership, among these expectations was that after being accepted they should be able to wait – at worst for almost four months – before actually starting the programme.

The Projects in Context

Pawson and Tilley (1997) argue convincingly that in the evaluation of any social programme it is essential to consider contextual and environmental factors as well as programme content and delivery. In the case of projects such as Freagarrach and CueTen, which necessarily rely on a sufficient number of appropriate referrals if they are to work with the intended target group, a key factor in their success or failure is their ability to establish their credibility and worth in the minds of social workers, teachers and police officers at all levels in their agencies. The contexts in which CueTen and Freagarrach were established differed in ways that turned out to have a long-term impact on the projects' work, and therefore need to be considered here.

Action, Not Words: Establishing CueTen

Apex's original proposal contained nothing on the proposed location of the project, and the Scottish Office's only requirement was that it should not be in Central Region, where it had just provided funding for Freagarrach. The idea of siting the project in Fife came relatively late in the planning process, but made sense to Apex because it was already running projects there, had links with the police, the local authority (especially the Social Work Department), and local employers, and had suitable premises in Glenrothes. As noted above, Apex staff also hoped that the consequences of local authority reorganisation would be less disruptive in Fife than elsewhere, since the new authority would have the same boundaries as the old Region. But in some respects the proposal was relatively undeveloped: for example, it was vague about the relationship the new project would have with existing facilities and organisations. The programme depended on the cooperation of other agencies, since much of the work, especially in the second block, was to take place away from the project base, and the proposal stressed complementarity with existing services and mentioned 'consultative discussions with potential partners' in the delivery of the programme. At one stage the possibility of a joint project with another non-statutory organisation was considered, with Apex as the prime contract-holder, but it was eventually decided to proceed with Apex as the only non-statutory organisation involved, and that its partnership should be with the local authority.

In late 1995 Apex staff worked on raising awareness of the project and building its credibility in a series of presentations to the middle tier of management in the police, social work and Education, and contacts with the Reporter and Children's Panel members. They found a particularly sympathetic response from the Director of Social Work, whose style of maximum action, minimum paper, fitted well with Apex's own, and who had encouraged a developmental view of social work with young offenders that was hospitable to voluntary organisations. The relevant agencies had already made a conscious effort to coordinate their response to children in difficulties, establishing a Childcare Strategy Working Group to encourage and facilitate cooperation between departments, in particular Social Work and Education, whose recent relationship had been notoriously fraught. The tensions between them were a main theme of the 'Kearney Report' (Scottish Office, 1992), which concluded that 'the relationship between the two directorates was unsatisfactory to a degree far beyond that which might ordinarily be expected' (paragraph X.4). The Director of Education had been, in particular, critical of moves by the Social Work Department to close residential establishments for juvenile offenders, without (in his view) proper consultation, and their closure was said to have left Panel members with inadequate resources at their disposal. In interviews about the development of the CueTen project it was repeatedly emphasised that it was impossible to understand the inter-agency politics of Fife without taking this history into account; equally, the reorganisation which was largely complete by the time the research began was said to have laid the foundations for a new start, since staff changes at the top of the relevant departments had consigned the old conflicts to the past.

It seems clear, however, that when Apex was working to establish the new project and the links with social work and Education which were essential for its functioning, relationships between the two departments, at least at senior level, remained strained; and it did not help that at times schisms appeared between sections of the same department. Local authority staff spoke of a 'general atmosphere of suspicion and mistrust', and of the feeling that any idea that came with a recommendation from the Director of Social Work would automatically be rejected by the Director of Education. At the same time, 'the local authority reorganisation was announced and people started moving'; but although this promised improvements in the long run, it created immediate difficulties and complications for Apex: valued relationships were lost and new ones had to be built – in particular, the reorganisation meant that Apex lost its close and mutually respectful relationship with the Director of Social Work. The advantages associated with the relative stability of Fife's administration were therefore not as clear-cut as Apex, and perhaps The Scottish Office, might reasonably have imagined: the legacy of old conflicts made agreement and cooperative action between Social Work and Education difficult, and personnel changes meant that the network of contacts that Apex had envisaged at the beginning of the project was disrupted.

The Childcare Strategy Working Group, including senior representatives of Social Work and Education, seems to have been one of the few settings in which a consistent effort was made, from 1993, to develop a coherent inter-agency strategy. (Interviews suggested that it helped that the staff chiefly involved were both English, and therefore – it was implied – were more accustomed to inter-agency cooperation; but it may have been more to do with the fact that both were new to Fife.) One of the Group's main concerns was the development of the resources needed to make sense of the policy that children should be diverted from residential care and supported in the community; another was how to reduce exclusions from school. Group members were frustrated, however, by the apparent lack of enthusiasm from the Director of Education, to the extent that some members felt its ideas were not as widely disseminated in schools as they could have been, and the group found it difficult to make direct contact with any sympathetic school rectors (headteachers), who might have provided the impetus for change. New tensions began to appear as social work representatives became impatient with what they saw as the lack of action from Education. In this context Apex's style of going ahead rather than engaging in endless talk, and of finding allies outside the formal decision-making structure, was a risky one.

The result was, in the view of some social work staff, that 'the project was established before all the procedures and the practical issues had been resolved'. The same view was widespread, in a stronger form, in the Education Department, which, it was generally felt, had been excluded from discussions at the planning stage. To some staff it seemed that the new initiative 'came onto the scene very quickly as if from nowhere'; even within the Strategy Group, which had been discussing the need for just such a scheme, some members were surprised when it was presented as 'all cut and dried'. This lack of initial involvement was still being referred to in interviews two years after the first young people had started at CueTen. The practical effects of the speed with which the project was established seem to have been mainly on its links with schools. For example, although there had been a meeting between Apex staff and school rectors in October 1995, the key representative of the Education Department on the Strategy Group (who was likely to be accepted as credible and authoritative) was not able to present the new developments to the rectors until January 1996, when ideally 'it should have happened the previous summer'. Although the proposals received a generally positive reception, some practical issues remained unresolved. The basic practical question of who should pay for the young people's transport to the CueTen project remained a matter of contention between Apex and the Education Department for almost two years. Education staff also raised questions about the effects of removal from school for six months of 14 and 15 year-olds during what is notionally a coherent two-year course involving both coursework and examinations, and about whether attendance at the project would be monitored in the same way as attendance at school. In practice, this proved to be a non-issue, since most of the young people who attended CueTen were not in any meaningful sense removed from school in order to do so; they were not attending school in the first place.

There is of course another view of the matter – Apex's; from its point of view, the only way to establish that something works is to get it up and running. In the words of one member of Apex senior management:

> There is too much time and money wasted in setting up projects too slowly, trying to make sure that every thing possible is taken into account. Our target was to start on 23 October; we were ready but Social Work and Education were not.

This in effect meant that while the project staff were in place they had no young people to work with. From Apex's point of view, the reasons for the failure to start work when planned included the reluctance of some social workers to appreciate what a 'non-social work' organisation had to offer, the disruptions caused by internal reorganisation and staff changes, and the general lack of enthusiasm (with a few exceptions) on the part of the Education Department. Apex staff, used to dealing with Further Education colleges and other training providers, were not prepared for what they saw as the conservative and slow-moving character of the school system in Fife.

In the nature of the case, there is force in the arguments of both sides. Perhaps Apex should have spent more time in communicating fully with all parties, and especially with the Education Department, given that the experience staff already had of working in Fife should have sensitised them to the particular importance Education attached to being fully consulted about social work initiatives. On the other hand, it is surely right that it is impossible to agree every last detail in advance of starting work, and there is no doubt that many good ideas for projects have foundered in a sea of talk. In discussing the work of the Safer Cities projects in England and Wales, Tilley (1992) distinguishes between 'masculine' and 'feminine' institutions and approaches to change. The terms refer not to the gender of participants but to the qualities archetypically associated with men and women. Both approaches, according to Tilley, have virtues and vices: an organisation with a masculine style will be good at getting things done, but may be perceived as threatening and thus alienate potential partners; a feminine style is more likely to gain cooperation, but entails the risk that the organisation working for change will be seen as irrelevant and thus become marginalised. Apex, one could say, adopted a masculine approach to the establishment of the CueTen project, with the benefits and costs which this entails. In the circumstances – in which, in the opinion of one local authority employee, 'the project has gone ahead against a background of almost discouragement' – there may have been no alternative. And it should be stressed that most people who attended the introductory meetings at which Apex presented its plans responded favourably to them. There was, after all, little dispute that some additional community resource for juvenile offenders was needed. As one Assistant Reporter commented,

> the Panel Members were very pleased that a new community-based resource was becoming available. There really are very few resources available for the Panel to consider, they sometimes don't know what they can do when someone starts to reoffend and they have already had all that's available.

Bringing People Together: Establishing Freagarrach

In contrast, the Freagarrach Project was from the outset explicitly the product of a partnership, although it was managed by Barnardo's Scotland, and its public face was (and is) that of a Barnardo's project. Those involved in the partnership, in addition to Barnardo's, were the then Central Regional Council (essentially, the Education and Social Work Departments), Central Scotland Police, and the Reporter's Office. The formal application for funding was from both Barnardo's and the Central Regional Council, and it was clear from interviews held at the beginning of the evaluation and from written sources that the convincing evidence that was provided of meaningful and well-established inter-agency co-operation was a distinctive and welcome feature of the application, and contributed substantially to its success. From both the interviews and the documentation it was quickly apparent that there already existed, prior to the specific development of Freagarrach, a high degree of inter-agency collaboration and co-operation within Central Region. There was open and formal dialogue between the police, the Social Work Department, the Education Department and the Reporter's Service; this had culminated in a well formulated and comprehensive written strategy, which was attached to the application to the Scottish Office.

The strategy was developed, supported and agreed by the chief officers of the four main agencies in partnership. Its focus and intent specifically related to the joint planning and provision of services for young offenders, coupled with the wider goal of community safety. It set out (Central Regional Council, undated: 1) the five key principles adopted by the four main services:

- to always act with the young person as a primary consideration;
- to share information with other services within the parameters of the law;
- to coordinate responses between services;
- to develop, together, a wide range of actions, treatments, disposals and responses appropriate to the different levels of need of such young people;
- to seek to divert young people from the criminal justice system where this was appropriate.

Our interviews revealed what key personnel believed were the main factors that initially brought the four main agencies together, and provided the focus for their collaboration. One important step was taken by the Chief Constable. Following complaints about a group of persistent offenders by a number of residents in Alloa, he initiated a meeting with the Chief Executive of the Regional Council and the other chief officers to discuss responses to the problem of offending by young people. As a result it was agreed to undertake an intensive local study, focusing on the town of Denny, on the relationship between offending and other adolescent behaviour.

Staff from the police, education and social work were seconded for a six-week period in order to carry out the study. Their report, which became known in Central Region as 'The Denny Youth Study', appeared in the autumn of 1993, and, according to the strategy document (Central Regional Council, undated: 1), its findings 'caused the four key operational services... to start to jointly address the issues of youth offending in Central Region'. While the strategy document describes the results of the Denny study as 'in no way remarkable', one result which had important outcomes, and was cited several times in the interviews, was that there was a stronger relationship between offending and exclusion from school than between offending and truancy (cf. Graham and Bowling (1995), for example, which suggests that offending is strongly related to both).

The Denny study was seen by the interviewees as a powerful catalyst for an inter-agency approach to young people's offending. At the same time, there were important changes in personnel among senior officers and elected members. Historically, it appeared that there had been very little co-operation between the agencies at senior officer level. The Departments of Education and Social Work were reportedly (from both sides) critical of each other in a style described as 'banter but with an edge to it'. There were also tensions between senior officers and elected members. In the 1990s officer-member relationships were said to have improved, along with inter-agency relations, as a result of changes in the composition of the Council: as a one-party state in miniature, Central Region had sometimes been known as 'Albania', and the arrival of Labour councillors with a 'modernising' outlook had helped to reduce what one interviewee called the 'isolation' of chief officers. A new Chief Executive was able actively to promote a more 'corporate inter-agency approach'. Furthermore, there were changes at senior level in each of the main agencies, which were felt by many interviewees to have led to important changes in operational style and ideologies; according to one, 'the physical change in personalities was important together with changes in perception'. The promotion of a corporate approach by the Chief Executive was actively welcomed, adopted and supported by the new chief officers, and corporate agendas were quickly seen as the way forward. This shared belief that corporatism rather than separatism was likely to be more effective in dealing with young offenders reflected government policy of the time:

> The Government consider that there is considerable scope for improved multi-agency collaboration in providing effective services for children who present special problems in the development of normal personal self-control. No agency − school, social work, psychological service or police − is solely responsible nor does any hold all the answers (Scottish Office, 1993, para. 7.26).

This statement was reproduced on the inside cover of the important *Report of the Working Party into Juvenile Crime* (Central Scotland Police, 1994), which contains significant proposals for developing a management strategy for dealing with juvenile crime. Together with the general content of the report, it indicates the prominence of the inter-agency approach in the thinking and operational strategy of Central Region Police. The Chief Constable and the Director of Social Work were seen as those mainly responsible for initiating the inter-agency commitment to develop a joint strategy and were described as the main partners, certainly in the early stages. The then Director of Education described herself as 'open to this kind of interchange and co-operative work,' and was receptive to the idea of the police as potential allies. The principle of inter-agency working and its rationale were also accepted by the Reporter, although the potential for inter-agency conflict was illustrated by his concern that decisions to divert young people from the formal system should remain within the Reporter's ambit rather than passing to the police.

Differences are to be expected and even welcomed in inter-agency responses to offending, because the personnel and agencies involved have quite properly different interests and priorities; total agreement on everything is not to be expected, and would hardly be healthy if it occurred (Pearson et al., 1992). What matters is how the inevitable differences and occasional conflicts are acknowledged and managed. Our interviews led us to conclude that the process of interaction during the early stages of the development of a common strategy for young offenders in Central Region allowed differences to be discussed honestly and openly. In the words of one interviewee: 'People were able to talk openly about their concerns... the [chief officers'] group enabled grouses to be expressed and then to be swept away'. The grouses were aired in a setting where all were motivated to find a basis for agreement: the group 'came together to find a common purpose'. At the same time Central Scotland Police, through the new TRACE computer system, were able (and, importantly, were willing) to share comprehensive statistics on patterns of juvenile offending within the region. The importance of these statistics in identifying and defining the key issues emerged in the joint strategy document (Central Regional Council undated: 1−2), where they were used to provide a rationale for the agreed target areas to be addressed by the Chief Officers. The key facts as presented in the strategy are set out below:

- most offenders only commit one offence (69 per cent);
- a further group of young offenders only commit two offences (10 per cent);
- a substantial amount of juvenile crime (19 per cent) is committed by 1.6 per cent of the juvenile offender group;
- there was, it appeared, a relationship between exclusion from school and offending;
- the most crime prone young people were boys aged 13 and 14;
- [it would appear] that offending was a 'normal' behaviour pattern for up to 30 per cent of male people within the Region.

The same statistics, in a more comprehensive and sophisticated form, appeared in the *Report of the Working Party into Juvenile Crime* (Central Scotland Police, 1994), as an important factor informing police policy and practice. They provided reliable data specifically relevant to understanding the problem of youthful offending at a local level, and the police were willing and indeed eager to make the benefits of TRACE more widely available. While facts very rarely speak for themselves, the experience of Central Region suggests that local research, statistics and knowledge are likely to be an important element in any attempt to develop a coherent inter-agency strategy for young offenders. Locally generated data are likely to be more readily accepted than national figures over which relevant participants feel no sense of ownership, and provided that there are opportunities for their meaning to be discussed, as was the case in Central Region, they can provide an essential empirical underpinning for agreement on strategy. The main strategic issues agreed by the chief officers were as follows: 1) a decriminalising response to first and second time offenders; 2) an enhancement of services for offenders referred to the Reporter; 3) the provision of more intensive services for persistent and serious offenders; and 4) the creation of a database for tracking offenders and for evaluating the effectiveness of services in reducing offending behaviour. It is likely that the existence in Scotland of a consensus on the desirability of a welfare-orientated response to young offenders was important in enabling the chief officers to reach agreement on these principles.

The prevailing philosophy of the police's approach to juvenile offenders in Central Region was, in the Scottish context, a traditional one: an emphasis on 'need not deed', with primary consideration being given to the welfare needs of young offenders rather than to their punishment. Among other things, this meant that young people who offended together would not necessarily be dealt with in the same way; the decision would be based on an assessment of individual need, not on the nature of the offence. This adoption of a child-centred position was wholly consistent with the views of Kilbrandon as enshrined in Part III of the Social Work (Scotland) Act 1968. An integral part of the police's community safety strategy was what two police interviewees described as a return to 'old fashioned policing values with modern technology'. The approach of the police recognised, in line with previous research (Thorpe et al., 1980; Rutherford, 1986) as well as with the TRACE data, that the majority of young people who offend grow out of crime and that often the formal systems set up to deal with offending behaviour can exacerbate the problem. Equally, the commitment to providing intensive services for serious or persistent offenders (but for them only) could be supported by research from elsewhere, and was in line with the 'risk principle' (McIvor, 1990) that intensity of intervention should be proportional to the risk of reoffending. The police view was therefore that more young offenders committing minor offences could be diverted from the formal system of referral to the Reporter and be dealt with informally. The TRACE system facilitated the retrieval of aggregated data in a format that provided useful and usable knowledge about the processing of juvenile offenders, and their offending profiles. An interface between TRACE and a welfare database allowed for quick identification of any problems in a young offender's background which might suggest, even in cases of minor offences, that help should be offered. The new technology thus enabled a more targeted approach to policing and, in the Chief Constable's view, provided an answer to the Audit Commission's (1993) criticisms of untargeted and unfocused policing. The police were particularly interested in the development of targeted responses for the more persistent and serious young offenders, feeling that the practice of diversion, by impacting on the number of requests for reports from the Social Work Department, would free up the system to provide more innovative and intensive services for the persistent offender.

Two other elements of Central Scotland Police policy on young people who offend deserve to be mentioned, since they were emphasised by interviewees and indicate just how ambitious the strategy was. One was a concern to make community resources more accessible to young people and thus enable them to find legal means of getting access to exciting activities. The feasibility of this depended on the development of an accessible register of local facilities for sport and leisure, and the availability of local volunteers who would, when necessary, help diffident young people to make use of them. Another proposal was that when young people in residential care offended within the care establishment the first response of care staff should be to deal with the problem as parents would usually deal with difficult behaviour by a child at home – that is, they should try to resolve the matter within the home, and calling the police should become a last, not a first, resort. This would give a helpful message to the young person concerned – 'This is your home' – and save the police from time-consuming involvement in negotiating some resolution of the offence, the usual result of which would be a return to the care establishment.

The ideas put forward by the police (diversion, decriminalisation, systems management, and a continuum of services to reflect variations in the seriousness of offending) were apparently readily accepted by the Director of Social Work; he was familiar with such ideas from his knowledge of juvenile justice in England and Wales, where they were the basis of policies of diverting young offenders from a criminal justice system seen as more likely to produce harmful than helpful outcomes. While the same view of the formal system as inherently damaging would be inappropriate in Scotland (a point to which we return in Chapter 5), the Director of Social Work was reported to have said that the Children's Hearings System (CHS) could be a 'blunderbuss' or a 'rifle' (only the latter being capable of hitting the intended target), and, employing a different metaphor, that 'if you go around dredging the river you will pull up mud' (a variant of the familiar image of net-widening). The Reporter, in describing the CHS, believed that 'in the past it has been a blunderbuss', even if a 'benign' one, and that historically the Reporter had 'dredged up the mud'. Statistics of which the Reporter was aware suggested that practice in Central Region could be criticised for over-interventionism: the Region had, over the years, the highest rate of referrals to the Reporter on offence grounds per 1,000 children aged under 16 years (Scottish Office, 1995) – although a high detection rate could also contribute to a high referral rate. While sensitive to the dangers of shifting discretion from the Reporter to the police, the Reporter was, then, broadly in sympathy with the basic philosophy of the emerging inter-agency strategy.

Historically, a focus on young offenders has been marginal to the central concerns of Education Departments, and it is important to highlight the willingness of Central Region's then Director of Education to become an integral member of the inter-agency partnership. While, understandably, no formal statement on policy towards young offenders seems to have come from the Education Department, the Director reacted openly, positively and promptly to the developing strategy, and was keen that her department should contribute to what she saw as an interesting set of ideas. She was interested in the link between school exclusion and offending suggested by the Denny study, and was aware that Central Region had historically had the highest proportion in Scotland of children excluded from school. She was conscious that there was no 'comprehensive picture' of the work of the Reporter and no system of prioritisation, and that the Reporter relied heavily on school reports (often of doubtful quality) to help identify those at risk. Two practical initiatives which contributed to the young offender strategy flowed from these concerns: a policy of avoiding exclusion where possible was introduced, and to support headteachers in implementing it teachers of children with special needs were involved in training mainstream teachers in the management of challenging behaviour; and two teachers were seconded to the Reporter's Department as Education Liaison Officers, with a brief to work with teachers to improve the quality of school reports and to intervene directly with children, their families and their schools in appropriate cases.

One attraction of the overall strategy was that it was designed to have a positive impact on agency workloads by reducing them (the Education Department is a possible exception). It was inherent in the strategy that routine intervention in response to minor offences should be avoided or minimised, allowing for better use of existing resources and creating the possibility of developing new, well-focused services for those most in need of them. Another important element was the agreement to share information with other services within the parameters of the law, and the speedy and economical processing of information via readily accessible new technology was seen, particularly by the police, as essential to the strategy's implementation. Making information available to all means that no one agency can exercise the power which comes with privileged access to knowledge; in the field of criminal justice policy, this agency is usually the police (Pearson et al., 1992), so the enthusiasm of the police in Central Region for the TRACE system, and their wish that others should be equally enthusiastic, was essential to the development of trust and the sense of a partnership between equals. Although the police clearly provided the initial catalyst for inter-agency working in Central Region, their role was not seen as a dominant one. There was thus no basis for resentment that the other agencies were being incorporated into a police agenda.

Conclusions

The circumstances in which the two projects were established had lasting effects on the way they worked and the extent to which they were able to achieve their aims, leading to continuing difficulties in the case of CueTen, and to success in sustaining focus and direction in the case of Freagarrach. It is therefore worth trying to understand what factors in their origins were associated with these differences in their later development.

CueTen was an ambitious and innovative project which, in the minds of its sponsors and supporters, held out the hope of pioneering a new direction for social programmes for young people in trouble. Its parent organisation, Apex Scotland, promised a distinctive approach that was neither social work nor education, but something akin to the 'social pedagogy' (Hämäläinen, 2003) which features in the social programmes of many European countries as an integral part of policies for social cohesion and reintegration. CueTen's basic aim, to reduce the likelihood of further offending by increasing young people's chances in the labour market, was thoroughly compatible with the commitment to social inclusion (Stern, 1996) that emerged in government policy not long after the project was established. But the very fact that CueTen was different, that it was attempting something never before systematically tried in work with young offenders, meant that its acceptance as a resource for social work and education had to be worked for; it could not be assumed. There were also some specific, local issues that complicated the process of CueTen's integration into the range of services for young people in Fife. There is no doubt that the project suffered in its early days from a legacy of mistrust and suspicion between the Social Work and Education Departments. It may also have suffered from the speed with which it was established (or what some influential members of its constituency saw as speed), although it is certain that if Apex Scotland had attended to all possible bureaucratic and professional sensitivities its establishment would have taken much longer. As a result of the interplay of these factors, CueTen never became as embedded in the structures of inter-agency relationships, or in the minds of some relevant professionals, as it needed to be if the staff were not to feel a constant pressure to remind others of the project's existence and purpose. It could never rely on a spontaneous flow of appropriate referrals, and was therefore exposed to occasional temptations, largely resisted, to accept young people who did not fall within the designated target group. The project had to accept young people whose motivation to succeed was fragile at best, and this, combined with the heavy expectations placed on young people by its ambitious six-month programme, meant that the drop-out rate was a continuing issue. These problems are explored in subsequent chapters.

The ground was much better prepared for the establishment of Freagarrach. Interviewed five years after the first young person had begun to attend the project, its first leader reflected that in most respects the decisions made in establishing it had proved to have been the right ones over the longer term. Access to TRACE was crucial in enabling the project to remain focused on the intended target group; staff had sometimes worried that Freagarrach had been established as a response to an atypical period of juvenile offending in central Scotland, and that the estimate of 58 young people who met the basic criterion of persistent offending was too high, but even at times when the number of referrals dropped TRACE provided an indication of continuing need. It was helpful that the original staff were given time to 'develop an ethos' for the project's practice – 'care and control were embedded in practice before we were inundated' – and the principle of voluntary attendance had been vindicated by experience. The support of senior staff in the different agencies, a product of the joint strategy, had also been important, although the project still had to establish credibility with fieldworkers. The fact that the project's staff included people who were already known and respected in the area had been helpful in this respect. Another virtue of the planning for the project was that it had been explicitly intended to operate according to 'What works' principles (McGuire, 1995): its practice, instead of developing in line with staff or organisational preferences and interests, was to be based on the findings of effectiveness research. The fact that evaluation was built into the project's work from the beginning 'was a big bonus, though it made us nervous… it made us sharper and sensitised the team to the importance of self-evaluation'. As a flagship project, Freagarrach was intended to contribute to the dissemination of good practice, and there was evidence of success in this through staff involvement in conferences and the fact that many workers from other parts of Scotland had visited during its first five years; the model had, however, not been consistently promoted at central government level as an indication of how practice should develop.

On the other hand, some aspects of work which it had been hoped to develop remained unexplored, and some of the more ambitious elements of the original Central Region strategy had not materialised, leaving Freagarrach more isolated than originally envisaged. Work on victim-offender mediation had not developed as originally planned, as a result of the absence of good evidence to inform practice in this area with juveniles, which led to nervousness about the sensitivities of Victim Support and other interest groups. The original strategy had assumed that SACRO would receive funding for a mediation and reparation scheme for young offenders, but this never materialised (Bayes, 1997). Work on helping young people to move on after their time at Freagarrach had been satisfactory when they were moving on to further education, but less so when the intended move was into employment or training, as was increasingly the case over the 5-year period. In retrospect it would have been useful to have had a team member from the outset with expertise in employment and training, or a worker with a specific brief to liaise with employers and arrange work placements. In general, the project might have been planned to include a greater element of joint working on the programme with staff from other agencies (this had happened to a limited extent with the police, Victim Support and court staff), but the fact that more such work had not been undertaken was a reflection of the strains on other agencies rather than of reluctance to share work on the part of the Freagarrach staff: 'it was easier to do it ourselves'.

Other staff interviewed towards the end of the evaluation, in the Freagarrach team and in other agencies, expressed similar views. They highlighted as important the values and attitudes of the staff team, their evidence-based approach to practice, and the support provided by inter-agency commitment to the project, particularly the sharing of information by the police. This required 'bottle' from the police point of view, given the existence of a 'tradition in the Scottish police of not trusting social workers' (the original strategy envisaged that TRACE data would also be made available to the Reporters and to Education Department staff, but this was never achieved, because of the cost of installing the required computers (Bayes, 1997)). The importance of a genuine commitment to working in partnership was mentioned by several interviewees, particularly in relation to the police: while it was easy to pay lip service to partnership working, it was rare to see the principle realised in practice. Although Freagarrach had always – and rightly – been conceived as a resource among others within a coherent overall strategy, it remained important, according to interviewees from education and social work, that the project should be 'more embedded in people's thinking about resources…You can't do too much work in embedding awareness'. A directory of resources, which might have helped in this process, had been envisaged in the original strategy, but this (like the SACRO project and the wider sharing of TRACE data) had never materialised.

One theme of the evaluation of Freagarrach was to consider whether it would be feasible to replicate it elsewhere. While accepting the argument of Tilley (1993) that true replication of any project is impossible, we have tried in this chapter to describe some of the key 'mechanisms' (Pawson and Tilley, 1997) which can plausibly be identified as important for Freagarrach's success. We return to these issues in the concluding chapter, where we also consider changes in the broader environment of juvenile justice in Scotland, which help to explain why, despite its reputation as a successful project, there has in fact been no serious attempt to replicate Freagarrach.

In summing up the contrasting situations in which CueTen and Freagarrach were established, we can say that CueTen's arrival was met with suspicion in some important quarters, while Freagarrach was welcomed as an organic development of an existing, widely accepted strategy. CueTen arrived in an environment characterised by inter-agency suspicion, the product of a history of conflict, Freagarrach in one where inter-agency co-operation had been fostered and worked at to an unusual degree. CueTen was perceived as different, strange and unfamiliar, Freagarrach as a promising extension of ways of working that were known and understood. As a result, CueTen risked isolation from the agencies – the social work and education departments, the Reporter's administration and the police – upon whose support it necessarily relied, while Freagarrach was integrated into the work of these agencies, and was in part a product of their efforts. Finally, CueTen was committed to a single way of working, which, while intuitively promising, was novel and therefore untested, while Freagarrach could both appeal to the then emerging findings of research on effectiveness and show that it could vary its methods according to the demands and needs of individual cases. The histories of the two projects might have been foretold, in broad outline, from a consideration of these features of their origins.

Chapter 2

CueTen at Work

Freagarrach was evaluated over five years from August 1995, and CueTen for three years from May 1996, making it possible to track developments over time. The brief for the evaluation was similar for the two projects, and specified five main elements: an analysis of the projects' origins and establishment; an evaluation of process; an analysis of outcomes, including evidence of impact on subsequent offending; a cost-benefit analysis; and an overall evaluation which was to include an analysis of the projects' influence on practice elsewhere. In both cases the evaluation began with a close reading of relevant documentary material, interviews and discussions with people who had played important roles in the conception and establishment of the project, and close observation of the project's work with young people. This was followed by interviews with the young people themselves, members of their families, and project staff. This approach to the evaluation of process was maintained throughout the research period, and key staff were re-interviewed at the mid-point of the evaluation and towards the end. This chapter discusses the work of CueTen; the work of Freagarrach is discussed in Chapter 3.

The Referral Process at CueTen

CueTen was initially funded on the understanding that it would aim to work with 32 young people a year, organised in four groups of eight; in practice, although the total numbers were close to the target figure, there were three rather than four intakes a year, since four starts would have placed excessive strain on the staff, and left little room for staff training and development, or for holidays. After the first intake in January 1996, three groups started in the course of each year, at intervals of three to four months. The final group (the ninth) started in September 1998, by which time 86 young people had started to attend the project. The normal start of the referral process was for a social worker to telephone the project to establish whether a vacancy existed at the appropriate time and whether the young person in question met the criteria for acceptance. In practice, the criterion of persistent or escalating offending was not rigidly defined: the staff's rule of thumb was that a figure of three offences in the preceding year counted as 'persistence', but this was not always adhered to. Over 80 per cent of the young people who attended the project, however, had been charged with three or more offences in the previous 12 months, and where this was not the case other factors, such the young person's being 'at risk and beyond parental control', were taken into account. Other criteria were also interpreted flexibly: for instance, the first young person to be offered a place on the programme was already in residential care, not just 'at risk of residential care', but his place was agreed as part of a plan to prepare him for leaving care. Furthermore, some of the young people were accepted onto the programme without an appearance at a Children's Hearing, although in most of these cases a Hearing was pending.

The next stage in the referral process was the assessment interview. Normally, the young person was taken to the project by his or her social worker, with a parent or carer, for a discussion with project staff and an explanation of the aims and purpose of CueTen. If necessary, a member of the CueTen staff would accompany the social worker to the young person's home for the initial interview. The staff tried to minimise delays in the assessment process, seeing this as consistent with 'the Apex culture'. The virtues of a straightforward and reasonably quick referral process were also appreciated by social workers:

> I can phone up and arrange an interview on the spot, get the kid's interest and then develop it, build on it. If we have to wait weeks or even months they totally lose interest. You must have the kids on your side, you cannot force them to do anything they don't want to.

> If the process is time-consuming you can lose the window of opportunity, a downward spiral can take over.

But, since CueTen operated on the basis of 'closed' groups (that is, groups with a fixed membership), and there were only three starting dates a year for new groups, these comments only make sense in the context of social workers' awareness of when groups were due to start. A referral made at the 'wrong' time, just after a new group had started at CueTen, could be processed quickly in the sense that a decision on the young person's suitability could be made, but at worst it could be almost four months before he or she actually began to attend the project. Although it is possible that social workers were deterred from referring potentially suitable young people by the prospect of a long wait before they started at CueTen, no such cases were mentioned during interviews. Nevertheless, there is an obvious tension between the principle of closed groups, with a fixed membership and duration, and the need, as perceived by social workers, to strike while the iron was hot – that is, to get a young person accepted at CueTen at a time when he or she was showing some willingness to change.

Among the criteria for acceptance at CueTen was that the young person should indicate a willingness to attend and show that s/he understood what was expected – regular attendance at the project over a 26-week period; but sometimes this 'willingness' and agreement to meet the responsibilities of the programme were less than whole-hearted. In fact, the language of assessment and selection suggests a rather more rigorous sifting of referrals than normally took place. In reality, the assessment or selection process was usually little more than a fact-gathering exercise culminating in an offer of a place on the programme. Referrals to the project never arrived in sufficient numbers for the project staff to feel they could refuse any broadly plausible candidate; and we identified only a small number of cases which were prima facie suitable but did not become referrals. Most of the intakes were under- rather than over-subscribed, and as a result staff offered places to young people who turned out to lack any serious motivation or intention to attend the project on any regular basis, like the one who candidly said: 'I'm only attending so that it will look good at my panel'.

Even when the prognosis was not very bright, and there were obvious warning signs, as when an initial assessment interview had to be cancelled because the young person had absconded, or when individuals were described as 'sullen and uncommunicative' and the like in the course of the assessment, places on the programme could be offered. Not surprisingly, young people accepted for the project with such levels of commitment often did not complete the programme. This was a continuing worry for the project staff, although most of the social workers who referred young people to the project took a more relaxed view: since its client group consisted of some of the most difficult young people in Fife, it could not be expected to succeed with everyone:

> Some are getting referred because we don't have any more alternatives, and if they get the benefits [of attending the project] for at least some of the time, then that is OK from our point of view.

The messages young people received from their social workers about what to expect from CueTen, and what the project would expect from them, were also a relevant factor in shaping motivation and commitment, an issue to which we will return in Chapter 5.

Towards the end of 1997 the CueTen staff organised a series of awareness-raising seminars, to remind relevant professionals of the content, aims and referral criteria of the programme, and in the hope of encouraging more referrals. The seminars specifically aimed at social work staff produced a response that was disappointing to the CueTen staff, but those arranged for educational staff attracted far more of an audience. As a consequence of the interest displayed by the local schools, and in particular by their guidance staff, the number of referrals increased, mainly coming directly from schools rather than through the designated route, via the Social Work Department. This placed the CueTen staff in a dilemma: they welcomed the increase in the number of referrals and the opportunity it gave them to be more selective, and wanted to respond positively to the new interest being shown by schools. On the other hand, some of the young people referred clearly did not meet the agreed criteria, and the established referral procedures did not include direct referrals from schools. After discussion, it was agreed that referrals from schools – mainly from guidance teachers – should go first to the Social Work Department, where their suitability for CueTen, particularly in terms of their offending, would be assessed. The episode illustrates a consistent theme throughout the life of CueTen: the need continually to promote the project in order to stimulate enough appropriate referrals.

CueTen at Work

Here we consider the programme of work offered at CueTen and the processes involved in delivering it, starting with the young people's first contacts with the project. The young person and their parent or carer would initially meet some of the project staff as part of the referral process, normally visiting the premises to get an understanding of what the project had to offer and what expectations staff had of young people attending the project. The young people were then given an opportunity to reflect on what they had been told, and were handed a leaflet that outlined the structure of the programme and contained the statement of agreement to the conditions of attendance at CueTen which all young people had to sign if they were to be accepted onto the next intake.

Young people were, then, asked to make a choice about coming to CueTen; but it was a choice made within serious constraints, and there could be no guarantee at this stage of the authenticity of their commitment. Some felt that they had no real choice:

> I have a panel pending, I don't want to get put away, the social worker said this would help, that the panel wouldn't be so strict if I was coming here.

> If I didn't come here I would get put away. Social worker didn't say that, but I knew it.

Some (but a minority) of those whose initial agreement was somewhat half-hearted, or who saw attendance at CueTen as the lesser of two evils, went on to participate actively and even to enjoy what the programme had to offer:

> Originally I wasn't too keen on coming here, but it's good; the work is so different from school, and it might be useful.

Generally, however, initial lack of motivation was a good predictor of subsequent difficulties.

A strikingly repeated theme of interviews with young people was that almost all had very negative attitudes to school, sometimes to the point where almost anything would have been preferable:

> I chose to come here rather than school, but I wasn't sure what we'd be doing.

Even after initial visits, discussions and explanations, many of the young people had little real idea of what to expect from the CueTen programme, or what it would expect of them. Gradually, folklore and gossip began to develop, and young people who came after the first year or so of the project had often heard something about it beforehand; they would mention a friend or relative who had been in an earlier intake and had reassured them that they would find it bearable, or even on occasions enjoyable. Their understanding of what would actually take place at CueTen remained rudimentary, however: several said that despite what they had been told they still thought that it would be like school, and they were invariably pleased when they discovered that it was not:

> I thought this place was going to be like school but with *more* discipline, thought I'd be sitting in a classroom. I didn't know it was going to be so much to do with getting work; I hadn't read the leaflet.

In contrast with their experience of school, the young people found the CueTen staff willing to listen, available to discuss problems with them, and polite and respectful. The project's achievements in this respect were recognised by guidance teachers:

> Apex can work with the 15-year-old disaffected with school; they may even do similar 'work,' but it is not in a school, they are not restricted by all the rules of a school.

The 26-week programme at CueTen originally started with a 13-week block which involved daily attendance at the project. The young people were collected from their homes in the morning, normally by taxi, and returned at the end of the session. Following an induction period, during which they were introduced to the programme, and essential rules and health and safety information were explained, they embarked on a training programme designed to help them learn through active participation. The individual components, or modules, were delivered in group settings, and covered skills and topics such as drawing up a personal skills inventory, the value of training and employment and the barriers to participation, how to deal with authority and conflict, and how to disclose relevant issues from the past. The staff aimed to help the young people develop realistic and reasonable attitudes, towards social life in general and towards training and employment in particular. On occasions this part of the programme was extended, to allow the staff to continue working with young people who did not seem ready for external placements, or who were particularly reluctant to attend work or college.

The first few weeks of the early intakes proved to be a difficult time for some young people not used to having to abide by any routine, so the staff – who were always willing to adjust their style of work in the light of experience – decided on the gradual phasing-in of attendance on the fifth intake, in an effort to make the initial experience of attending CueTen less daunting. The young people were expected to attend for two days in the first week, with one day added each week until full-time attendance was attained. On the whole they found this gradual build-up helpful and preferable to an immediate expectation of full-time attendance. The staff also found the later intakes generally more manageable, with their more gradual introduction to CueTen and the time this gave the young people to adjust to their new circumstances and take in new information. This induction phase was also intended to give both parties a chance to decide in a more measured way whether attendance at the project was desirable, or even feasible. Staff hoped that it would allow the young people to make a more informed choice, by giving time for ideas and expectations to be clarified: those who positively chose to continue would then be more committed and have a greater chance of completing the programme. As we explain later, there is little clear evidence that this aim was achieved: failure to complete the programme remained common, despite, in some cases, intensive efforts to re-build interest and commitment through meetings and discussions with social workers and family members.

The differences between what CueTen expected of the young people and what they had been doing previously were striking: very few had been following anything like a normal routine of regular education before starting at CueTen. Some were described by their social workers or project staff in terms such as 'virtually out of control.… not doing anything positive', and 'not having basic social skills… don't get them at home'. Throughout the programme the project staff had constantly to address these issues, encouraging the young people to reflect on their attitudes and their behaviour, and its consequences, potential and actual, for themselves and others. Their attitudes to offending and their general anti-social behaviour were constantly challenged. They were encouraged to take responsibility for their own actions and to reflect on behaviour which had led to damaging situations, in particular their abuse of drugs or alcohol. Much of this work was at best only indirectly connected with employment or training, and one of the earliest and most important discoveries made by the staff was that these young people were generally neither able nor willing to work steadily through a structured formal curriculum, as a group of well-motivated older offenders (like those with whom Apex had worked elsewhere) might have done. Group processes required constant attention, if the content of the programme was to have any impact. Nevertheless, the project staff also tried to stress that the young people did have positive qualities and the capacity to change their circumstances. The CueTen staff were certainly not the first adults to tell them that they needed to change some of their attitudes and forms of behaviour, and in particular that they must learn what behaviour is appropriate to what setting; but they may have been the first to convey to the young people that they themselves could have a positive input into the process of obtaining work, or into training as an introduction to work. For some young people, this meant that educational work at CueTen was more acceptable than it had been at school.

An inherent part of CueTen's work was to connect the young people with resources in the community, particularly further education colleges and local employers. This entailed trips away from the project base, and other contacts were made through guest speakers who visited the project, including careers advisers and police officers. These visits were sometimes marred by the hostility and suspicion of the young people, but they were calm and orderly compared with many of the trips to local employers and with the young people's participation in 'taster' sessions at the local colleges. College staff acknowledged that the appearance of the CueTen group on college premises had been a learning experience for them and their colleagues: although committed to widening participation, many staff felt that they had never encountered young people quite as unmotivated as those from CueTen. Over time, suitable and willing college staff were identified who could cope with the groups' behaviour, but not all organisations were able to adjust in this way: one training organisation that provided team-building exercises for the early intakes withdrew its services, finding the behaviour of the young people too difficult to manage. Recreational activities outside the project produced fewer problems of disruptive behaviour, and came to occupy part of almost every day of attendance at CueTen. Staff regarded these as an incentive to participate in training and as a reward for good behaviour, but they had a relatively greater importance in the minds of the young people: when recommending CueTen to prospective new group members, their friends and relatives invariably mentioned the opportunities it gave to play pool or go ice-skating rather than to learn the principles of equal opportunities or telephone interview techniques. The staff, while sensitive to the possible criticism that they were rewarding bad behaviour, regarded these recreational outings as helpful in establishing group norms and identity, and in setting levels of acceptable conduct in various public settings. It was clear, too, that these trips helped staff maintain control, and gave them some relief from the immediate pressures of managing the group.

Everyday life at CueTen was, then, rarely relaxed or harmonious. Although the staff were adaptable and highly motivated, and their achievements with some young people were recognised and welcomed by social workers and others, there were persistent problems of group management and control. The staff were simply not prepared for the level of disruptive and erratic behaviour they had to cope with, nor was Apex Scotland organisationally equipped to provide them with the kind of support that might have helped. The programme was planned to provide a coherent training and skills development curriculum, but the volatile nature of the groups and the possibility of erratic individual behaviour created a constant air of unpredictability, which some external organisations − and, often, the CueTen staff themselves − found difficult to manage. Things rarely went to plan: carefully planned sessions could be and were totally disrupted by the actions of one young person who, for reasons which might be unrelated to anything happening at CueTen, could not or would not co-operate with the staff or other group members. In such situations the staff withdrew young people from the group to allow them time to cool down, or to talk over whatever was troubling them, while trying to minimise disruption to the main group work programme. They sought to make time to respond individually to young people who were angry or distressed without neglecting the overall needs of the group − a difficult, and sometimes impossible, balance to maintain.

Problems of a different kind made it difficult to deliver the programme of blocks two and three (in practice, a single block), which was intended to put into practice the individual training plans developed in the first block. This required part-time attendance at the project, work and college placements, and, if appropriate, a negotiated return to school. In practice, the process of developing realistic plans and implementing them often proved to be very time-consuming. Despite the effort devoted to providing work experience, which was of course central to Apex's aims and approach, the number of successful work placements was small. Staff had to negotiate with young people who might have been content to attend the project, but were not prepared to attend a work placement, or who were so restrictive in their requirements as to make a successful placement almost impossible to find. Others declared an intention to attend, only to walk out after a short while or fail to return for their second day, while the behaviour of others − a minority − was so disruptive and erratic as to make them unsuitable for any work setting. The staff, in response, tried to be realistic in their assessment of the young people's motivation to follow their individual training plans, a process which took up the first few weeks of the second half of the programme, but the original assumption that young people could and would move on at this stage into training or further education often proved mistaken: even young people who had successfully completed the first phase of the programme were not necessarily prepared to continue their progress away from CueTen.

In the rare cases in which work placements did prove successful, this was enthusiastically recognised by those responsible for the young people's supervision as 'a real result' − an achievement that held out the prospect of a long-term change in their life chances. The local employers who agreed to be involved were (perhaps by definition) positive in their attitudes towards the young people, even those who were not very committed or prepared to persevere with the placement. Some employers continued to demonstrate their support and willingness to 'try again' in the face of almost constant failure. The view of most such employers was that as long as involvement with CueTen did not interfere with their prime business function they were willing to try to help; successful placements included a local garden centre, tyre and exhaust centres, the dockyards at Rosyth, and a local car-dealership. Successful returns to school were even rarer: young people with negative experiences of school (that is, virtually 100 per cent of those who attended CueTen) were unwilling to see going back to school as a progressive rather than a retrograde move, and some were quite explicit that they had no intention of ever returning.

In the second half of the programme the young people were expected to attend the project on one day a week (increased to two days after the first intake) for individual counselling and group work. They were also encouraged to get involved in some local community project, as part of CueTen's commitment to trying to improve their self-esteem. Projects included a rock concert to raise funds for a local charity, a sponsored pool marathon for the benefit of the Cystic Fibrosis charity (chosen because one group member had a relative suffering from this condition), and the painting of a mural on a wall in a local day centre. Although these community projects were time-consuming and sometimes difficult to manage, staff thought them worthwhile since they encouraged a sense of community involvement and introduced the young people to the idea that others could benefit from their efforts; they were also a way of putting into practice the team-building skills introduced in the first part of the programme. The young people had to work together as a group, communicate and negotiate with each other in a reasonable manner, make decisions and establish collective goals, agree specific tasks for individuals, and work to agreed schedules, if the projects were to be successful. Not every group became involved in such a project, and levels of commitment inevitably varied, but most of the young people who did become involved were at some stage committed and enthusiastic.

To summarise this account of the content and style of work at CueTen: the programme as originally envisaged required substantial adaptation in practice. Derived from Apex's experience of working with adults, it proved too formal, too tightly structured, and too concerned with content rather than process, to be fully applicable to the juveniles who came to CueTen, generally with negative experiences of and attitudes towards education (and sometimes with no recent experience of it at all), often from disrupted and unhappy family backgrounds, and (almost by definition) heavily involved in subcultures of delinquency. The staff had constantly to adjust and adapt: the crucial movement was away from a rational model of formal education and training to a recognition of the less rational elements of individual emotion and group processes – to something much more like social work, with both individuals and groups. While aware of the importance of family relationships for the young people's motivation and behaviour, the CueTen staff were not in a position, given the location of the project on a single site and its Fife-wide catchment area, to develop regular or formal work with families; nor is it certain that they would have had the skills or resources to do so. The staff often felt, too, that they had to cope with the demands of the young people, and adapt their practice accordingly, very much on their own: they were expected to manage, to get on with things without the expectation of the kind of support and supervision that is institutionalised in many social work agencies. The CueTen staff often found their work stressful and draining; and they had to manage the stress largely without support from their own organisation.

Duration and Intensity of Contact

Since it was meant to work with the most persistent young offenders in Fife, the supervision provided by CueTen was supposed to be intensive, and the extent to which this was actually so was one of the questions for evaluation. Formally, the programme was meant to start with daily attendance by the young people; with the first group this meant attendance for four full days and one half-day, but, recognising the need to have time for satisfactory assessment, development and self-appraisal, the staff introduced a second 'free' half-day for the second intake. The basic hours of attendance for full days were 10 a.m. to 3 p.m., including a supervised meal break; the two half-days involved attendance between 10 and 12, giving a notional normal level of attendance of 19 hours each week. As mentioned above, the staff altered the attendance requirements for the fifth intake, but the nominal weekly hours remained the same. In practice, the notional 13 weeks of the first block were sometimes extended or contracted to accommodate holiday periods and to take account of the fact that in some groups the young people had started at different times. Because of such contingencies as staff training days, public holidays, and various acts of God such as snow blizzards and high winds, the possible period of attendance in the first block ranged from 52 to 68 days, and for most young people was about 60 days. In terms of hours, this gave a notional total of about 225 hours of direct contact with the project and its staff during the first phase of the programme (well in excess of the recommended minimum of 100 hours over six months derived from research on effectiveness by Lipsey (1995)). It is not surprising that many young people found it difficult to cope with the demands of this ambitious programme, and that actual rates of attendance were often very different from those formally required.

By the end of October 1998, 72 young people had been at CueTen for long enough to have completed the full 26-week programme. Of these, 29 (40 per cent) were judged to have actually to have completed it, although this did not always mean that they had attended very assiduously: the attendance of those who formally completed the first block ranged from 22 to 67 days. Another ten young people completed, or virtually completed, the first part of the programme, so that 54 per cent of those who started in the first seven intakes spent at least 13 weeks in reasonably close contact with the project. The staff were disappointed by the rate of non-completion, but it was probably not out of line with what should have been expected from other studies. For example, Lucas et al. (1992: 12; see also Raynor and Vanstone 1996) reported an overall completion rate of 62 per cent (75 per cent when non-completion for benign reasons is excluded) for the STOP probation project in Mid Glamorgan, which was considerably less demanding than the CueTen programme in terms of overall duration and intensity of attendance required (STOP entailed a total of 35 two-hour sessions and attendance twice a week, giving an overall duration of about 4½ months). Lucas et al. (1992) suggest that a combination of personal problems, low motivation and further offending can produce an attrition rate of around 50 per cent, and note that completion rates for offenders aged under 21 were somewhat lower than for the older group. It should also be remembered that participants in the STOP programme faced the prospect of a return to court, and the possibility of a much more severe sentence, if they did not maintain a satisfactory level of attendance, whereas the young people at CueTen had no such incentive. In the light of these considerations, the completion rate for CueTen, though below what was envisaged and lower than the staff would have wished, need not be taken as firm evidence of failure. More recent and much larger scale research on programmes for adult offenders in England and Wales has reported a non-completion rate of about two-thirds (Hollin et al., 2004), and in comparison the CueTen figure begins to look almost respectable.[1]

Twenty-six young people left the project either as a result of their own decision or because their behaviour outside the project led to changes in their circumstances, such as a move into secure accommodation, which made their continued attendance impossible. The reasons for leaving varied: of some young people it is possible only to say that they showed very little interest in or commitment to the programme. Three attended for only one day, two for two days, and one for three; in these cases, it is likely that a more rigorous assessment by the social worker would have concluded that a referral to CueTen was not appropriate. But there could be positive as well as negative reasons why the programme was not completed: three left at the age of sixteen, or just before, to take up jobs, a provisionally positive outcome in Apex's terms. Less positively, three of the young people who left absconded from residential or foster care, and therefore failed to continue at CueTen; and another three had recurring problems with placements in care that made attendance at CueTen, and indeed residence in Fife, impossible. Another identifiable group consisted of six young men who failed to finish the CueTen programme essentially because of their continued high level of offending, leading to periods in custody or secure accommodation. Two young men stopped attending ostensibly because of problems at the project.

The same could be said of the 20 young people who were 'permanently' excluded from the project (which did not always rule out the possibility of a further referral), sometimes after a few days, sometimes after several weeks, for acts of violence against staff or other group members, threatening or abusive behaviour, vandalism, drug use or generally disruptive behaviour – or for any combination of these. The exact circumstances which led to exclusion varied, but violent or abusive behaviour featured in at least ten cases: staff used phrases like 'uncontrollably threatening and abusive' and 'extremely aggressive' to describe the conduct that had led to exclusion. Two of these cases involved young women, one of whom threatened staff with

---

1 There are problems in making such comparisons, for example over what counts as starting a programme, what counts as attendance on any given day, and what counts as completion. The probation programmes in England and Wales are likely to have used stricter criteria than CueTen.

physical violence, while the other – already in care and subsequently placed in secure accommodation – assaulted another member of the group. Such aggression was invariably accompanied by a lack of commitment to the programme and disruptive behaviour of a less dramatic kind, which of course affected the concentration and commitment of other group members.

Such behaviour could itself lead to exclusion even when it was not associated with specific acts of verbal or physical violence. One young man, who lasted on the programme for nine weeks, was said by his guidance teacher to suffer from 'attention deficit syndrome;' he and a member of the next group, the fourth, were the subjects of frequent complaints from outside agencies, from which they were in the end effectively barred. In the second case, a company whose premises adjoined CueTen's called the police to have him removed from its property. Agencies visited by the young people at CueTen sometimes suffered acts of vandalism, as did the project itself: wilful damage to property was specifically mentioned by staff in their accounts of the reasons for exclusion of three young people, and certainly occurred in several more cases. In the later groups drug-taking became more explicitly a problem, and was the main reason for the exclusion of two young men, one of whom was excluded twice.

The overall picture that emerges from these accounts is of behaviour that by adult standards was drastically anti-social. To varying degrees, all these young people posed problems of management and control by their verbal aggression, threats of physical violence, actual assaults on group members, acts of vandalism and inability or unwillingness to focus on the tasks set by the CueTen staff. In some cases this behaviour was exacerbated by drug use. That so many of the young people attending CueTen should have displayed such behaviour is not surprising, given the strong association with delinquency of hyperactivity, short attention spans, a search for excitement, school failure and dislike of school and teachers, and experience of violence in the home (Farrington, 1997). Such problems did, however, come as a surprise to the staff in the early months of the CueTen project; they were simply not prepared, and not well equipped by their previous training or experience, to manage such behaviour. The constant adaptation to circumstances which characterised the development of CueTen was largely a response to behaviour that could have been foreseen, given that the great majority of these young people were genuinely persistent offenders and had long histories of educational failure. In particular, the original expectation that most of CueTen's programme would be delivered through group work on a formal curriculum was not realistic, as the staff soon recognised: many of these young people simply imported into the group at CueTen the kind of anti-social behaviour typical of delinquent peer groups, as described in a long tradition of criminological writing (for example Matza, 1964): bullying, threats, violence, lack of care and consideration for others or for the physical environment, and an impoverished level of oral communication. It is almost certainly the case that some of these young people were just not ready for what CueTen had to offer, and should not have been referred; for example, the guidance teacher who described the young man with attention deficit syndrome also thought that he needed intensive individual attention, which was not readily available in CueTen, though the staff tried hard to provide it.

Twenty-nine young people, six of them young women, completed, or virtually completed, the programme in the first seven groups. These young people were, in general, less persistent offenders before they came to CueTen than those in the other groups. Furthermore, to complete the CueTen programme required a substantial level of commitment, personal discipline and staying power; and although some of this group did not find it easy to maintain these attributes over the 26 weeks, all attended regularly enough and for long enough to suggest that they could, in principle, make the desired adjustment to the world of work. This was a much more feasible and intelligible aim than returning to school, as far as the young people were concerned; and none of the seven members of this group who were supposed to be reintegrated into school after their time at CueTen managed this without difficulties.

A tentative conclusion at this stage could be that CueTen's approach was, on its own, simply not suitable for the most persistent juvenile offenders; it was too demanding, too cognitively based and rational, for young people deeply immersed in offending, long alienated from the education system, from troubled and unhappy home environments, and in many cases with problems associated with drug or alcohol use. The staff had no real access to the young people's families; even if they had felt that they had the skills needed to intervene in family relationships in a systematic way, they could not have done so. As a result, problems in family relationships were never directly tackled by the project, and in many cases continued to disturb and preoccupy the young people, seriously reducing their ability to concentrate on the CueTen programme. It is possible that a programme like CueTen's should be thought of as most appropriate for young people towards the upper end of the intended age range – 15½ or older – who will not be expected to return to school, and whose family problems have been resolved (or at least reduced to a tolerable level), or ceased to impinge directly on their lives, as they move towards more independent living and leave the family behind. It may also be that to be effective a focus on employability should be linked with a broader service rather than being a programme's sole focus, a possibility hinted at in the following chapter, in the account of the convergence of Apex and Barnardo's at Freagarrach.

Chapter 3

Freagarrach at Work

The Referral Process

Referrals to Freagarrach came from social workers in the three local authorities – Clackmannanshire, Falkirk and Stirling – that made up the former Central Region, and were usually from teams dealing with children and families; towards the end of the evaluation period, seven referrals which resulted in acceptance came from criminal justice teams (reflecting the tendency for the average age of young people at the project to increase over time), and one successful referral was from a residential home run by a voluntary organisation. The project leader visited the relevant teams to explain the referral criteria and procedure early in the project's life, but the effort to ensure that social workers were aware of the project and understood its purposes was a continuous one, not least because of the rapid turnover of social work staff. Formal referrals were preceded by initial enquiries, usually by telephone, during which basic details were discussed and levels and patterns of offending were confirmed by the project staff. If at this point it was felt that the young person met the criteria for persistent offending, and that a referral would be appropriate, a referral form and an information booklet on the project were sent to the social worker. The social worker then discussed and completed the form with the young person and his or her parents or carers. The criteria for acceptance by Freagarrach were as follows:

1. The young person is aged 12–16 years [raised to 18 in 1999] at the time of referral to the project.
2. There have been at least five episodes of offending within the previous 12 months (i.e. a minimum of five charges from separate incidents), and there has been at least one episode within the last two months.
3. Offending behaviour is the main reason for any statutory agency involvement.
4. There has been a recent social work assessment that highlights the need for intensive support from the project.

Freagarrach also accepted referrals on young people who met these criteria and were in residential care outside the region, 'if the offending had been the primary reason for their removal from home' (Freagarrach Project, 1996: 4), and if they had somewhere suitable to live in the region.

As mentioned in Chapter 1, Freagarrach staff had direct access to the TRACE database of Central Scotland Police. Every week (barring failures of the IT system), the police supplied the project leader with a disk which enabled the project to update its own computer system. It also allowed information given on referral forms about charges, frequency and patterns of offending to be checked, and project staff often also checked information from social workers with the Reporter. Access to TRACE allowed the project to monitor the level of offending for all young people in the Central Scotland Police area (the former Central Region) up to the age of 16, and indeed the system could be used to highlight the young people with the highest number of charges at any one time. The project leader was therefore able to contact both the police and the Reporter to gather further information on young people listed on TRACE as having a high number of charges, but for whom Freagarrach had not received an enquiry or a referral; thus she was able to be proactive in pursuing possible referrals to the project, rather than having to rely solely on the judgement of social workers. In these cases, after checking details with the police and sometimes the Reporter, Freagarrach staff would contact the relevant social worker directly to discuss the possibility of a referral. This would not always be appropriate, as when, for example, the social worker was already working to a clear plan, and might have considered but rejected the idea of a referral; in other cases, when the idea of Freagarrach had not entered the worker's mind, this proactive approach was a means of ensuring that young people were not deprived of an opportunity to attend Freagarrach through simple inadvertence on the social worker's part.

During the period covered by the evaluation there were 209 enquiries about the possibility of a referral to Freagarrach, resulting in 144 referrals. In only 23 cases where the process reached the stage of a formal referral did it not result in a young person's starting to attend Freagarrach. In the period to 31 March 2000 there were 121 'starts' at Freagarrach, by a total of 106 young people: that is, 15 attended the project twice. The most common reasons why a referral did not result in attendance were that the young person did not meet the criterion of persistent offending, and reluctance on the young person's part to make a commitment to work with the Freagarrach staff. In the 65 cases in which enquiries did not lead on to referrals, the most common reason was again that the young person did not meet the criterion of persistent offending; in other cases, welfare issues rather than offending were judged to be the main problem, the referral concerned a child under the age of 12, or it was decided that another service should be provided. In a few cases, the social worker simply did not follow up the initial enquiry, and the case was not such a clear candidate for Freagarrach that the project leader pursued it.

The numbers of enquiries, referrals and starts at Freagarrach varied from year to year, but not in a readily identifiable pattern: for example, there was no evidence of an early burst of enthusiasm, or of gradually increasing interest in the project. The peak years for enquiries were the first, third and fifth, and this was also roughly true of referrals, although the year-to-year variation was smaller. Twenty-one young people began attending the project in the first year, 23 in the second, 27 in the third, 21 in the fourth, and 29 in the fifth (each year running from 1 April to 31 March). There were no significant differences over the five years of the evaluation in the proportion of referrals that led to a young person's attendance at Freagarrach.

The Freagarrach staff used the formal criteria for admission as a threshold or trigger that activated the project's interest in a case. Within the total population of offenders who met the criterion of five or more episodes of offending, the project tried to offer places to those with the highest number of episodes or with a worrying pattern of escalating offending. TRACE data allowed for an estimate of the size of the overall population of persistent juvenile offenders in the region at any one time – that is, those with five or more episodes of offending in any one year – and regular checks were undertaken during the evaluation to ascertain how many young people who met the criterion of persistent offending were not referred (or were not the subject of an enquiry) to Freagarrach. At no stage was there any evidence of a large pool of persistent offenders who were missed by the project's referral system. Where TRACE showed very persistent offending (ten episodes or more in a year), and thus suggested that the young person concerned should have been the subject of a referral, checks with the project leader revealed reasons why a referral had not been made (and similar reasons were present in the few 'very persistent' cases which were referred but not accepted). Typically, these young people were in residential care or secure accommodation for welfare reasons, or had no viable home base in central Scotland; others were unwilling to attend the project, had committed offences, usually sexual, of a kind that suggested a need for specialist help, or had produced a spate of offences over a short period and then apparently stopped offending. The evidence is, then, that the referral system, largely thanks to the project's access to TRACE data, worked well, in that very few potentially suitable cases were missed altogether, and that Freagarrach did not work with young people whose offending was not so serious as to meet the criteria for the target group.

The problem that CueTen experienced, of a long delay between referral and actually starting work on the programme, is liable to arise with any specialist project in high demand; this is obviously to be avoided as far as possible, especially since the referral may well have been triggered by a particular crisis. Although there were times when a wait for Freagarrach was inevitable, since the project was working to its full capacity of 20 young people, it was rare for the gap between referral and attendance to be longer than eight weeks: only ten (8 per cent of the total) such cases were identified. Forty-four (37 per cent) young people started attendance within less than a week after the referral, and a further 53 (48 per cent) started within four weeks. In the small number of cases where the wait was longer, project staff often tried to provide support to the young person and the social worker, in order to sustain hope, interest and motivation. Young people who were re-referred after attending the project were always taken back almost immediately, as the staff responded to an evident crisis. The fact that Freagarrach provided individualised programmes rather than running a series of closed, fixed-term groups allowed for this flexibility and meant that long waits (after which the original motivation, and perhaps the need, might well have been dissipated) were unusual.

It is important to note here, after the mention of the project's informal work with young people, that those who were not formally accepted onto the Freagarrach programme were not necessarily deprived of all that the project had to offer. Fifteen cases were identified of young people, including two young women, who never appeared as having attended in the project's formal records, but who nevertheless received some service from Freagarrach – and there were almost certainly more cases than this. This 'hidden' work is hard to quantify, but its existence means that the figure of 121 'starts' on the Freagarrach programme underestimates the project's overall workload, and the number of young people to whom it provided some help. This work arose from the staff's commitment to offering a flexible service to young people in crisis and to supporting social workers who had identified a need. The work was often described as 'outreach', meaning that a Freagarrach worker would visit the family home; the first case of this kind was recorded in early 1997, and work lasted for around four months. Typically, the aims were to work on the young person's offending and to provide support to the family, in the hope that with relatively short-term, low intensity involvement a crisis might be prevented from developing into a long-term problem. In other cases the project arranged for support to be provided via a volunteer, the young person attended family meetings at Freagarrach without participating in a formal programme, project staff supported other workers with their specialist expertise, and the social worker was able to use the project's resources to enhance work with the young person. The effectiveness of this type of work in reducing offending is impossible to measure, but there is no doubt that it was perceived as helpful by social workers, and won for the Freagarrach staff a reputation for adaptability and responsiveness.

Freagarrach at Work

Once a referral had been accepted, the project leader or a senior project worker visited the young person's home, and the young person and his or her parents or carers were invited to visit the project base at Alloa or Polmont, whichever was nearer home. This allowed them to see the project building and to meet the team member who had been allocated the case. The reasons for the young person's referral to the project were explained, and s/he and the family were given details about the project and its programme of work. Project staff explored the young person's views, interests and expectations, and set out their own expectations of young people attending the project. Mutual expectations were similarly explored and clarified with the parents or carers. All being well, it was at this point that the young person was considered to have started to attend Freagarrach, and the programme of work began immediately after this initial process of engagement.

The basic expectation was that every young person should have three direct, face-to-face contacts with the project every week during the period of attendance, each contact lasting between 1 ½ and 2½ hours. The guideline period of attendance started off as six months, but, as will become clear, in practice the project operated with a good deal of flexibility, and the average length of stay was never as short as this. Every young person was given a timetable of meetings. When they were due to attend the project, young people were collected from home by a project worker, who would also take them home after the session. Those who lived nearby, or were attending the special educational facility that shared its premises with the Freagarrach's Polmont site, made their own way to the project. If staff felt that specific circumstances warranted closer supervision or increased intensity of work, they negotiated more frequent contacts.

The first 4–6 weeks were used as an assessment period, in which the project staff could begin to understand the specific needs and circumstances of each individual, and to explore the reasons for their offending and related relevant problems. At the end of this period there was a contract meeting, at which a formal contract document was agreed, highlighting 'the key issues and tasks to be undertaken' (Freagarrach Project, 1996: 9). This meeting was attended by the young person, his or her parent(s) or carer(s), the allocated project worker, the young person's social worker, and any other professionals involved in the case. The meeting was held at the appropriate Freagarrach site and chaired by either the project leader or a senior project worker. The contract document was agreed and signed by all in attendance, and minutes were taken of the discussion, the tasks to be undertaken, and the future roles of the people involved. The contract covered the objectives the project was to pursue with the young person, relevant to the explicit aim of reducing the individual's offending behaviour. These objectives related to the five main areas of work that were established at the outset (Freagarrach Project, 1996: 9): offending behaviour; victim awareness and reparation; education and employment; family issues; and constructive use of leisure time.

This document, known as the Individual Programme Contract, was a 'working tool' (Freagarrach Project, 1996: 9) which specified the foci of work for each individual and informed the nature and content of the specific methods of work adopted. For example, a young person's offending might be associated with involvement with a peer group, with drug or alcohol problems, with family tensions, or with problems at school, and one or more of these would be identified in the Individual Programme Contract as requiring particular attention. This document served as the basis for regular reviews or Progress Meetings, which were held approximately every eight weeks following the initial contract meeting, ideally with the same personnel, or at least with the same agency representation, as at the initial contract meeting. Progress was assessed in relation to the objectives contained in the initial contract or agreed at any subsequent Progress Meetings. The work undertaken with each individual was described and discussed and, in conjunction with a review of current case details, the future programme of work was agreed. Minutes of each Progress Meeting supplemented the Individual Programme Contract to ensure that the objectives of work remained relevant and feasible. At the final Progress Meeting a closing summary was produced, recording the achievement or otherwise of the objectives within each identified problem area.

The project staff worked with young people individually and through formal group sessions, as well as less formal group activities. In the main, individual sessions involved the young person and his or her allocated project worker, but another member of staff could stand in, and at times two staff members would work with one young person. The primary focus of the individual work was offending: discussions related specifically to the situation, motivation, perceptions and circumstances of the individual's offending pattern. While the immediate situational context of offending behaviour was central to this work, it also incorporated exploration of wider contextual factors, such as education or employment issues, family relationships, use of leisure, and any other personal and social difficulties. Though fully aware of the research on effective practice with offenders, and committed to the methods and styles of working suggested by its findings, the staff also recognised the need to work flexibly and responsively to the needs and aptitudes of each young person, rather than attempting to impose a single undifferentiated programme on all.

Formal group sessions were used to discuss specific topics within the five main areas of concern, and dealt with these in general terms rather than exploring the situation of one specific individual. Other formal group work activities, instead of being topic-based, were organised with the aim of bringing the young people together to develop their personal and social skills in peer interaction, trust, decision-making and taking responsibility. Less formal group activities were aimed, at one level, at providing opportunities for enjoyment, but also at encouraging the young people to develop an interest in activities that might lead to a more constructive use of leisure time. Achieving success in challenging activities was seen as a means of enhancing self-esteem, and the sharing of the experience enabled workers to build and strengthen their relationships with the young people. The staff also recognised the importance of involving parents in their work: meetings were arranged at Alloa or Polmont to which the parents or carers of all young people currently attending the project were invited. In principle these meetings were held at regular intervals; in practice they varied in frequency, depending on the level of parental interest and on staff resources. As a by-product of the meetings, some parents at one stage formed a group of their own, with the encouragement and support of the project staff, to which speakers were invited to address topics highlighted in group discussions. Some mothers continued to attend the parents' group after their son or daughter had left the project, finding in it a source of support not available elsewhere.

Before looking in more detail at the various components of the programme, it is worth saying something about the style and approach adopted by workers in the project: the manner in which a programme is delivered may be as important for success as its content (see, for example, McNeill et al., 2005). Lewis and Gibson (1977) approach this issue by drawing a distinction between 'engagement skills' and 'work skills'. They argue that in analysing client-worker interaction it is only possible to say that work is taking place if there is a clear agenda, understood by both parties, and that the interaction is relevant to this agenda. 'Engagement' refers to the process of helping the client to define the agenda and to work within it; it is not a once and for all achievement which can be forgotten once the client has formally signed up to an agenda, but a process which needs to be continually reiterated, since at any time and for any reason clients may be unable or unwilling to work on the agreed agenda, and the worker's task is to 're-engage' them. The process of engaging young people in work is less tangible to researchers than that of working with them (in Lewis and Gibson's sense), since it is inherently complex and raises questions about workers' styles and skills in communication which can only be answered by subjective judgement and interpretation. Worker style has, however, long been recognised as crucial to the success of interventions (Truax and Carkhuff, 1967), and it became apparent during the evaluation that in the view of the young people and their carers the way in which staff related to them was a crucial element of the project's success in motivating young people to attend initially and in retaining their enthusiasm for continued attendance.

The workers' style was both informal and informative. From numerous visits to the project and discussions with workers, it was clear that the overall approach was strongly client-centred, and that the views and wishes of young people were sought throughout: the flow of information was in both directions. The workers were unanimous in their belief that the positive aspects of a young person must always be identified and highlighted (in line with the principle of reintegrative shaming that the act, not the actor, should be condemned (Braithwaite, 1989)). This was interpreted by the young people as 'respect' (for the importance of perceived respect in relationships see Scheff (1997)). The positive personal attributes of the workers were described by young people and their families in terms that suggested general qualities such as friendliness, helpfulness, humour and honesty; and workers were also seen as available. These are everyday human rather than professional attributes, and it is worth remembering their importance, especially given the increasingly technical language and emphasis of research on effectiveness.

Flexibility applied both to the management of the programme and to workers' approach to individual young people. From the workers' perspective, this was important as a means of maintaining a balance between the requirements of the planned programme and an appreciation of the young people's wishes and feelings. Moreover, the concept of balance indicated an ability to share some of the control and direction of specific sessions or work plans, and an emphasis on the achievement of objectives through skilled negotiation rather than by demanding compliance (in line with the principle of voluntary attendance). The approach was described by one of the workers as follows:

> [It's] important to build a positive relationship. I found a lot of positives in his life. Also wanted it to be seen that he had to work. I wanted a balance between the two. I had to lay it on the line early on so he would not have false expectations but I would have jeopardised the relationship if I was critical or lectured him. Flexibility is a question of balance – prepared to fit in with changes the young person might want, but also aware that they might manipulate.

Whilst the approach left room for the views and interests of the young people, it was also clear that the workers retained ultimate control, though not through simple enforcement, and that the relevant work was usually completed.

Many, perhaps all, of the young people at Freagarrach had been the object of negative judgements and opinions, from people in the community, professionals such as police officers and teachers, and often from members of their own family. Freagarrach could not avoid the negative aspects of young people's lives and behaviour, which were after all the reason for their attendance, but in recognition of the burden of negative evaluations the young people carried staff tried to identify and build on their positive qualities and the positive elements in their lives. Again it was important to achieve a balance: if the focus was always on the things that were 'wrong' with the young people and their lives, this would be unhelpful in attempting to raise their self-esteem; on the other hand, the things that were wrong were the target for change, and could not be denied. As one worker put it: 'we get in the mud with them to get them out again'. A further aspect of the approach was the willingness of staff to persist in engaging young people in the face of difficulties or apparent lack of enthusiasm and commitment. The message, as one worker put it, was that 'I won't go away'. The reality of this approach in practice was evident throughout the research. On occasions, usually within the first few weeks of the programme, some young people went through periods where their motivation to attend began to wane.

In these circumstances the workers continued to visit the home, and acted as if they assumed that the young person would return to the project. If the young person was not at home, workers would often visit other places in an effort to maintain contact (the project's contact sheets recorded meetings in, for example, shopping centres and supermarkets).

Work on offending constituted the central component of the Freagarrach programme. The starting point was generally a discussion of all the charges against the young person recorded in the TRACE system or, for those aged 16 and over, in their criminal record. The immediate situation of offending was explored, together with the young person's accounts and explanations, in order to gain some insight into both the situational reasoning and the situational circumstances of offending behaviour. The focus was on understanding the cognitive and behavioural aspects of offending for each individual, and the initial task was to gain some understanding of the types of offences committed, together with the sequence of events leading up to them, which could enable the identification of possible characteristic patterns of behaviour and the typical situations in which these occurred. The young person and the worker would identify and explore particular factors which appeared to increase the risk of involvement in offending (for example, the presence of particular peers, the time of day, particular situational triggers, and so on). This cognitive-behavioural emphasis is among the key features of successful programmes for persistent offenders, according to the research on 'what works' (McGuire, 1995).

This aspect of the work was undertaken individually, and in most cases the interventions that followed were also on an individual level, adapted to the specific issues that emerged from each case. Usually workers spent time helping individuals to recognise and avoid or withdraw from certain situations, and empowering and enabling them to make different choices and decisions when faced with similar situations in the future. The emphasis was always on the need for the young people to take responsibility for their own actions and their consequences for themselves and others. Using the situation of offending as a starting point, workers could begin to explore other contributory factors that are known to be linked to offending. In particular, for some young men at the project, drug or alcohol misuse played a major part in their offending, and in these cases work concentrated on the causal links between substance misuse and offending.

The project provided opportunities for young people to explore their general perceptions and understandings of crime. The topic of masculinity was one important focus for group discussion, and the link between masculine reputation and offending behaviour was also explored on an individual basis when appropriate. Anger management was also included in the programme for young people whose offending was associated with difficulties in controlling their temper. Whilst formal counselling was the main vehicle for focusing on individual-level issues, this work was often carried over into less formal contacts: for example, all the workers mentioned the importance of the time spent with young people in car journeys to and from the project. Similarly, interactions with individual young people during activity-based sessions were seen as an integral part of the repertoire open to workers.

The approach at Freagarrach was eclectic in that it represented a practical synthesis of a number of cognitive, behavioural and social skills-based methods (specific influences included the work of Priestley et al. (1978); Denman (1982); Priestley and McGuire (1985), and Thorpe et al. (1980)). This allowed for the use of a variety of techniques and resources, including pencil and paper exercises, worksheets, video, role play, cartooning and the analysis of reasoned action, and staff tried throughout the evaluation to acquire new skills and methods and develop existing ones. Group sessions were used to explore designated topics in a more general way without focusing specifically on any one individual, though it was hoped that they would have an individual impact; for example, some sessions with older offenders invited them to consider the consequences of continued offending, with the aim of promoting constructive reflection. Early in its life, the project made arrangements with the social work staff at Glenochil Young Offenders Institution to set up a programme that allowed young people at Freagarrach to meet staff and inmates. The purpose was to provide 'an opportunity for the reality of custodial sentences to be discussed' (Freagarrach Project, 1996: 9), rather than being designed to shock or frighten the young people, which evidence suggests would have been counter-productive (McIvor, 1990; Lloyd, 1995). The work involved, rather, a shared discussion and an exchange of views, although the realities of institutional life and loss of freedom were no doubt conveyed in the process. The programme was in three parts: initially, staff and inmates from Glenochil visited the group at Freagarrach; then each young person had a short meeting with a Glenochil inmate; and finally, the young people met at Freagarrach to discuss the experience. A similar arrangement was later established with the women's prison at Cornton Vale.

It was always clear that the central core of the programme concerned offending, and that most of the intervention related to the specific criminogenic needs of the individual. In the detail of its practice, therefore, as well as in the broad structure of its programme, Freagarrach worked in ways that should be associated with positive results in terms of reoffending. Summarising research on effectiveness, McGuire (1995: 15) points to the importance of separating 'client problems or features that contribute to or are supportive of offending, from those that are more distantly related, or unrelated, to it'. The cognitive-behavioural core of the work was also, as noted above, in line with findings on effectiveness, as were the wide range of techniques and methods used, and the project's recognition of the variety of offenders' problems. This entailed work on aspects of their lives known to affect the risk of offending though removed from its immediate behavioural context (for example Farrington, 1997): education and employment, family relationships, and the use of leisure time.

The original proposal for Freagarrach recognised the importance of education for young people, and, given the educational histories of the young people who attended (described in Chapter 4), it is no surprise that education should have been a significant part of the programme. A key aspect of the multi-agency development of a young offenders strategy in the former Central Region was the commitment by the Education Department to provide seven day unit places to young people at Freagarrach who were currently receiving no education and for whom integration or reintegration elsewhere was unlikely. The project did make use of these places, but this was only part of the work undertaken on education. There were three main types of intervention: advocacy and liaison, in which staff worked in partnership, mainly with teachers, educational psychologists and social workers, with the aim of finding or enhancing educational services for young people who were receiving little or no education; practical support for young people attending or being (re)integrated into a school or day unit; and work on the cognitive and behavioural aspects of young people's experience of and response to education.

All young people at the project could be placed, at any one time, into one of four broad categories: a) receiving no education, and with no link to any educational establishment; b) not attending, through truancy or exclusion, but retaining some link with a school or day unit; c) attending a school or day unit; d) about to leave school, or already left. For those in the first group, the primary focus was on exploring the possible educational options with the young person, their social worker, and the relevant Education Department staff. The day unit places offered by Education were mainly intended for these young people, but they rarely if ever found the move back into education easy or straightforward. Many of them had strongly anti-school attitudes, and had been out of the education system for a long period, following permanent exclusion for truancy or behaviour problems (in some cases these amounted to serious violence). Staff worked on developing the young people's commitment and motivation, discussed their expectations, and tried to prepare them, at a cognitive and behavioural level, for handling day to day interactions in a new educational setting. A similar approach was adopted for young people in the second group, the non-attenders, but here the emphasis was on exploring the possibility of (re)integration into school. This was often a gradual process, starting with part-time attendance at mainstream schooling and a day unit, but with the eventual aim of total reintegration.

The final group, which over time came to include a high proportion of the young people at Freagarrach, consisted of young people who had either left or were about to leave school. The project staff liaised with local colleges, training courses and careers offices on behalf of these young people, and in a few cases were able to arrange work experience placements (for example, in a pre-school summer playgroup and a local garage). Staff would explore possible career choices with these young people, help them to obtain relevant information, and support them in approaching relevant training establishments, agencies or businesses, for example with help in completing application forms and arranging appointments. Other work focused on skills and assertiveness training to help in gaining employment, and explored such issues as the differences between school and college, making friends, and advice on benefits and entitlements. In helping young people to move on from school the project staff relied heavily on local networks and personal contacts, which they worked hard to develop; but, as noted in Chapter 1, this was an aspect of work in which it would have been useful, in retrospect, to have had specialist knowledge and expertise from the start. Moving on to independence and life as a young adult remained a problematic process for many of the young people at Freagarrach throughout the period of the evaluation.

A significant aspect of the overall philosophy and approach of Freagarrach was the importance attached to establishing and maintaining meaningful dialogue with the young people's parents or carers. The project's own early account of its work highlighted the link between 'chaotic backgrounds' and persistent offending, the 'isolation' felt by many parents, and their need for 'support in coping with...

problems within the family which are compounded by the offending'. This was why 'the involvement and support of parents in the project is consistently sought and encouraged' (Freagarrach Project, 1996: 10). A high level of parental involvement in the formal referral process, and in the work on contracts and reviews, was evident from the minutes of these meetings and from observation: the views of parents were consistently sought and their comments heeded. Although the agenda and management of the meetings were controlled by Freagarrach staff, parents were positively encouraged to participate, and, while they were usually not as vocal as the professionals in attendance, they generally appeared comfortable and not inhibited from contributing. This formal contact at meetings was supplemented by less formal contacts with families throughout the programme, and families' experiences of these informal contacts must have helped them feel at ease and able to contribute in the more formal settings.

The project's records of contacts showed that when collecting young people and taking them home workers used the opportunity to maintain informal contact with their families, and interviews confirmed that this was deliberate practice: these home visits allowed staff to keep parents up to date with their children's progress and to give them a chance to talk about the family's current circumstances and concerns. The process of engagement with families was similar to that described with young people, and, as with their children, staff tried to stress the things parents were doing well, not just their failures and inadequacies. On occasions staff visited families on a more formal, planned basis to discuss a specific issue, the visits being instigated by the project or prompted by a request from the family. Project workers were very willing to respond to family requests for support, since, as one worker put it, 'parents are needy too'. The focus for most of the family contact was on improving relationships, developing more positive patterns of communication, sharing the different perspectives and views of family members, formulating and agreeing boundaries, encouraging consistency in parenting, and helping parents to recognise positives in their children – as well as offering general support. In a few cases more intensive, planned family work was undertaken over a number of sessions, often involving co-working with the social worker for the family.

The content and purpose of work varied. In one case work was undertaken with the families of two young people who were offending together; in another the project worker successfully encouraged a parent to start a college course. At one level the family contact was made with a view to making or sustaining changes likely to support the young person's commitment to desist from offending, but this did not preclude a response to the more general and personal needs of the family or a member of it. Inevitably the receptiveness of families to outside help varied, and much family contact was concerned with building sufficient trust for parents to accept the project and its objectives. The general commitment to involving families in the work was supported by parents' meetings organised by project staff. These meetings were held – at least in principle – every two months, and were designed to bring together all parents and carers of the young people currently attending the project. Staff provided transport if required. The purpose of the meetings was not to discuss individual cases but to give everyone a chance to discuss, in a general way, the problems faced by parents of young people involved in offending, and their feelings about the project. While not all parents chose, or were able, to attend all meetings, the overall level of attendance was high. The effort the Freagarrach staff put into engaging and involving parents was unusual for a project working with juvenile offenders; its value is likely to have been in reducing some of the feelings of isolation and self-blame to which parents of persistent offenders are liable, and it is also worth noting that support for parents is associated with reduced rates of offending (for example Farrington, 1996).

During their time at Freagarrach young people were given the opportunity to participate in a variety of leisure activities, at one of the project's two sites or elsewhere. As with other work, this could be on an individual or group basis. Activities included cooking, arts and crafts, music, swimming, go-karting, football, golf, cycling, fishing, pool, gymnastics, skiing, juggling, climbing, hill-walking and riding. One young person was referred to an art group in the community; another was introduced to a karate club; others attended 'taster' courses, for example in map-reading, at a motorcycle project, and in football coaching. While there was always a fun element to these activities, the serious purpose was to introduce the young people to new pursuits that they might wish to continue after leaving the project. Participation was also used as means of giving young people a sense of achievement, and of course was a vehicle for the staff to develop positive relationships with young people. Some activities, apart from being a possible introduction to a new leisure pursuit, were used to promote other, more specific aims. For instance, one young man was taken on a ten-mile hike by his project worker, which allowed for an informal but intense discussion about his offending, his family, and his future ambitions. Three young people were supported in planning and organising a three-day outdoor 'residential': the purpose was to develop in the young people a sense of responsibility for their own actions and towards the group in which they were working. A similar exercise was set up for four young men who were about to leave Freagarrach: the task for this group was to plan and organise a residential trip to the English Lake District. The aims, as expressed by one of the workers, were to 'consolidate the development of social skills outside the home environment and to develop a sense of commitment to organising and completing tasks', and to help the young men 'move on from Freagarrach'.

The project staff were fully aware that resources for young people in the community were limited, and that once they had left the project, they were likely to experience a dramatic reduction in the amount of adult support and encouragement available. The staff continually tried to identify potentially useful resources from agencies such as Community Education, but it often seemed to them that the only available resource was the project team itself. While the staff were strongly committed – in principle and practice – to supporting young people once they had left, they did not have the resources to undertake post-programme support for all the young people who might have welcomed and benefited from it. Freagarrach was always conceived as only one part of a larger strategy, and was not expected to compensate for a general lack of provision for disadvantaged youth in the community. There are indications from research on projects for offenders that work which is successful in the short term may need to be reinforced after the intensive part of the programme if promising early results are to be sustained (Raynor and Vanstone, 1996); the lack of guaranteed support for young people after they had left Freagarrach therefore represents not only a failure fully to implement the inter-agency strategy but a factor which could tend to reduce the prospects of successfully diverting young people from criminal careers.

Another element of Freagarrach's original conception that was never fully achieved concerned victim awareness and reparation. A key aspect of the individual offending work explored the effects crimes have on victims, thus encouraging the young people to think about the consequences of their offending from the victim's perspective. In addition, a three-day group work programme was set up which focused on the perceptions and feelings of victims of crime, and encouraged the young people to consider situations where either they or their family had been victims. Victim awareness was thus very much an integral part of the programme. At various stages staff held discussions with representatives of Victim Support, with the aim of involving victims or their representatives in work with the young people; these eventually produced some modestly positive results, discussed below. Before this, there were instances in which project staff suggested that young people apologise directly to their victims, directly or in writing, and helped them to do so; and in a few cases young people directly compensated a victim by paying for property damaged or stolen, or by returning stolen items. Young people also became involved in direct reparation by doing unpaid work for the victim; some indirect reparation was undertaken through involvement in unpaid voluntary work; and a band formed by young people at Freagarrach in the second year donated the proceeds of its concert to Victim Support. Nevertheless, reparation to victims did not develop to the full extent originally envisaged. This can be largely attributed to the failure of the SACRO victim-offender mediation scheme to develop, as described in Chapter 1, but it is not certain that the Freagarrach programme would have been enhanced had reparation or mediation become a routine element of it. Direct reparation is often difficult to negotiate with victims, and indirect reparation, if undertaken as a form of punishment, is not always meaningful to the offender. A more individualised approach to reparation, where the restitutive actions are negotiated and have a chance of being emotionally satisfying for the offender and the victim, is preferable to a blanket approach in which reparation may be experienced by the offender as punishment or humiliation, and by the victim as grudging compliance with a routine requirement (Blagg, 1985; Smith and Blagg, 1989).

Developments in Freagarrach's Practice Over Time

The aspects of practice discussed so far were established at Freagarrach early on and remained relatively stable over the five years of the evaluation; but there were important changes in the project's work over time, and these are discussed in the following section. The changes reflected the self-critical, reflexive attitude of the staff team and their openness to new ideas, as well as being responses to changes in the project's environment; but the basic principles and styles of work that were established at the start were consistently maintained. The stability and coherence of the project's approach were demonstrated when the original project leader left in

September 1998, and her departure was followed a few months later by that of the team leader at Alloa. These changes had a short-term impact on staff morale, but there was enough continuity, both of personnel and of skills and understanding, to ensure that the project's essential features remained intact. Such changes are inevitable in the life of any organisation, and in general Freagarrach enjoyed the benefits of stable staffing and a common philosophy.

Perhaps the most important of the developments in practice related to the issue of helping young people to leave the project in circumstances which provided some promise of continued support. Throughout the five years of the evaluation, but particularly in the earlier period, many young people found it difficult to leave the community of care that Freagarrach had become for them; equally, the staff were anxious about withdrawing help from young people for whom no obvious alternative sources of support existed. The question of how to help young people leave the project became more urgent for the staff over time, not because of any external pressure to meet the original target of working with 40 young people in each year but as a result of internal changes: a refinement of the selection process and efforts to build a planned leaving date into the individual programme devised for each young person. The staff came to believe that in the project's early months some of the young people referred and accepted had been too young to benefit fully from what the project had to offer: the younger the offender, the more likely he or she was to have a complex range of emotional, behavioural and family-related problems in addition to the specific problem of offending; and fewer of the younger group (under the age of 14) had the cognitive ability needed to grasp the point of work on offending, or to acquire any insight into their behaviour and experiences. Some of the longest stayers at Freagarrach were among the youngest when they started the programme; the length of stay was associated not so much with continued offending as with other problems with which Freagarrach was not really equipped to deal. If they had been referred later in the project's life, some of these young people might have received the kind of informal, relatively brief support described above, allowing the staff to focus the offending-related core of their work on the older age group. With the older group, planning for their departure from Freagarrach concentrated on help in establishing a basis for independent life as young adults, and was therefore concerned with employment and training rather than with a return to school. A regular 'leavers' group' was started in the project's third year to help young people identify and understand the problems they would have to face after leaving Freagarrach, and in the project's records a sharper focus on planning for the move on after the programme became evident in the project's case notes and records. It remained the case, however, that many young people found it difficult to leave a setting in which, perhaps for the first time, adults had treated them with care and respect; and in a few cases continued support for young people well after they had formally left the project occupied much worker time and energy. The Alloa site, located near the town centre, was easier to visit causally than the Polmont site, which was on the edge of town; but young people did not have to be physically present in order to generate work.

In October 1997 a resource appeared that briefly promised to provide substantial help in enabling young people to move on to something constructive after leaving

Freagarrach. This was the Forth Valley Young People's Employment Resource (FVYPER), which was managed by Apex Scotland and intended as a service for young people in their final year at school and disenchanted with formal education. The Freagarrach staff, along with others, felt that this project had been set up hastily and without much consultation (compare the account of CueTen's establishment in Chapter 2), but they saw its potential value as a means of helping young people move towards greater independence. Unfortunately, anticipated funding from the European Union failed to materialise, and the project lasted only until May 1998. Seven young people from Freagarrach started the FVYPER programme, though for various reasons only one completed it (and he spoke very positively about the experience). More typically, the young people who went to FVYPER from Freagarrach saw it as useful but would have preferred to stay at Freagarrach to work on employment-related skills. Freagarrach staff too, while critical of FVYPER for failing to keep them informed of young people's progress and of what they saw as a rather mechanical style of programme delivery, felt that in principle a programme like FVYPER's was exactly what was needed to help young people move on from Freagarrach in a planned and constructive way, and that the FVYPER staff had shown that they could learn from mistakes.

At various points in Freagarrach's first five years the staff considered the possibility of employing an outreach worker to help members of the leavers' groups increase their job skills, liaise with prospective employers, and support young people after their entry into work. Eventually, in February 1999, something like this role came into being, when Apex obtained funding for a scaled-down project, employing one worker – a former member of the FVYPER team – who was based at Freagarrach. The Apex worker dealt with young people on an individual basis and focused closely on issues specific to employment and training, without trying to make connections with work done previously at Freagarrach. About 15 young people from Freagarrach had had some contact with the Apex worker by the end of March 2000, showing that there was a demand for the service. Both the Apex worker and the Freagarrach staff recognised, however, that the young people found it difficult to sustain motivation and hope: 'the problem is keeping them in training, not getting them started'. For young people long excluded from the routines of education, even a basic 13-week training course could seem 'an eternity', and the intensity and complexity of 'underlying problems in the background' meant that there was a risk of 'setting them up to fail'. Some of the problems of CueTen thus reappeared in miniature at Freagarrach.

The Freagarrach staff were strongly committed to the principle of joint working with staff from other agencies, but felt that the amount of such work actually achieved was limited, because of strains on the other agencies' resources. In the case of Victim Support, however, joint working was constrained less by resource considerations than by concerns on Victim Support's part that its focus on victims' interests should not be compromised by the provision of a service to offenders. In Freagarrach's third year, staff began to explore the possibility of developing community service-type work, in conjunction with a community care social work team. They were aware, however, of the need to ensure that this work was experienced by the young people as productive and relevant, rather than punitive and stigmatising, and worked alongside the young people on gardening, painting and decorating projects in the local community. While the outcomes of this work were seen as positive, both for the young people and for Freagarrach's local reputation, staff remained keen to develop forms of work that might contribute more directly to enhanced victim awareness and empathy.

After protracted negotiation on this delicate topic, a representative of Victim Support agreed to contribute to the work of Freagarrach with materials used for the training of Victim Support volunteers. These included a board game and a video, both designed to promote empathy with victims and reduce the effectiveness of such techniques of neutralisation as denial of injury and denial of the victim (Sykes and Matza, 1957). Project staff saw this approach as a potentially effective and non-threatening means of instilling a sense of responsibility and remorse, and eventually, they hoped, of developing a conscience which would make further predatory offending more difficult. Victim Support also contributed to role-plays and to the simulated trial described below. The Victim Support representative interviewed towards the end of the evaluation thought that the role-play would work better with younger than with older, more 'cocky' offenders; she had been happy with the extent of Victim Support's involvement in Freagarrach's work, since it had not diverted resources from victims. Victim Support later gave qualified approval to direct victim-offender mediation, provided that this was done selectively, in cases where the victim genuinely wished to meet the offender. The Freagarrach staff were clear that the project did not have the resources to undertake such mediation on a regular or formal basis, but they did undertake direct mediation in a few cases, as when a staff member accompanied a young person to a shop, where he paid for stolen goods. Reparation, however, usually took the generalised form of work in the local community on projects of environmental improvement, as described above.

The breaking down of barriers between the project and other agencies was seen by Freagarrach staff as a major achievement of its work in 1997–98: they saw this as an expression at the level of practice of the commitment to partnership represented by the Strategy Group, and found that the young people responded seriously and attentively to contributions by visitors to the project. The police in Bo'ness and Alloa worked with project staff on a group work programme focusing on joy-riding, which included a visit to the police station to see a video and discuss its implications. The workers involved evaluated the programme in December 1998 and concluded that it had been useful in helping the young people to think more clearly about the consequences of car theft and the ways in which supposed friends in a peer group could exert an unhelpful influence on them. Another initiative in 1997 was the organisation of a simulated trial in Falkirk Sheriff Court. This was an effort to bring home to the four young people who participated the realities of the gulf between the Children's Hearing System and the adult court system; it also reflected the tendency for the average age of young people at Freagarrach to increase, which gave knowledge of the adult system added relevance. The exercise required careful organisation and the co-operation of the Sheriff, police officers, a specialist social worker, defence and prosecution lawyers, and members of the local Victim Support scheme, who played the parts of victims and witnesses. It was therefore an impressive example of inter-agency co-operation, but not one that could be expected to be often repeated. According to the young people involved, the experience was a salutary one.

Changes in Freagarrach's Environment

Just as there were changes over time in Freagarrach's practice, so too there were changes in the environment in which it worked. The most obvious, and the most predictable, was the abolition of Central Region as an administrative unit, but another event which had a serious impact, at least over the short term, was the tragedy of the Dunblane shooting in March 1996, the aftermath of which inevitably brought different priorities for the police and social workers. Even in the first interviews with the people who had played the key roles in drawing up the original young offenders strategy, it was obvious that many doubted that a global strategy could survive the disaggregation of the region into three local authorities, since this would entail a more local focus of interest, new structures and procedures, and substantial staff movement. In the interviews towards the end of the evaluation, this reorganisation was still viewed as the moment when the commitment to a common strategy came under the greatest pressure.

Interviews at the mid-point of the evaluation allowed for an assessment of the extent to which the original strategy, and the inter-agency and inter-authority commitment to it, had survived reorganisation. At about the same time the strategy was formally reviewed by the project leader at the request of the Young Offenders Strategy Group, which had been restructured earlier in the year in an effort to ensure full representation at chief officer level. Bayes (1997) identified staff changes following reorganisation and lack of resources as the key problems in achieving the agreed strategic aims, a view largely supported by the interviews. The impact of staff changes and internal reorganisation was not felt equally across the three authorities, but was especially marked in Stirling's social work service: an immediate effect of this was a decrease in the number of referrals to Freagarrach from Stirling, as staff operated in 'emergency mode', and over the five years of the evaluation Stirling made proportionately less use of Freagarrach than Clackmannanshire or Falkirk. Some of the staff newly appointed at senior level were initially sceptical of the strategic approach, questioning what added value it produced; but over time they became convinced, and in some cases proved among the strongest supporters of Freagarrach and the strategy as a whole. Some aspects of the strategy that failed to materialise because of lack of resources have already been mentioned; another, specifically associated with reorganisation, was a shortage of foster care places for young offenders and of accommodation for young people generally.

Some of the most obvious changes after reorganisation were in the education service. Bayes (1997: 10) noted that the original strategy document referred to a 'Reporters' Resource Team', which was not defined precisely but was usually taken to mean the Reporters themselves along with their administrative support and the two Education Liaison Officers, one seconded to the Falkirk Reporter's office, the other to Clackmannanshire and Stirling. When responsibility for funding these posts passed from the Regional Education Department to the new unitary authorities, the latter post ceased to exist: the view of some new staff in the education service was that it had been a product of the over-centralised, paternalistic (or even Albanian) approach of the old region, and that school-related problems were better dealt with by schools themselves. Regret at the loss of this post continued to be expressed, however, especially by Reporters; and the Falkirk post, which survived throughout, was regarded as highly successful, largely because of the personal qualities of the post-holder, in reducing the demand for residential care, and as a valuable resource for the Reporter. The anti-exclusion policy promoted by the old region was similarly seen as an over-centralised (and dubiously effective) response to problems that properly belonged with schools; the result was a more uneven pattern of provision across the three authorities, in which Stirling claimed the greatest success in enabling schools to reduce the number of long-term exclusions. Central government policy later came strongly to support a reduction in the number of school exclusions, and all three authorities claimed success in this; but the impact of any changes was not visible in the experiences of young people referred to Freagarrach, and it is a fact that a young person may be receiving no (or minimal) education without being formally excluded from school. Freagarrach retained the use of seven places in a special educational unit in Falkirk, and some of its young people also benefited from the flexible and responsive service provided by the Day Unit at Alloa; but the development of 'flexible' educational packages increased the need for clear communication between Freagarrach and schools or colleges about where a young person was supposed to be at any given time of the day or week.

The devolution of responsibility for discipline to individual schools also revealed some strains in inter-agency support for the diversion of minor offenders from the formal system. There were incidents in which the police returned to their school boys who had been involved in a fracas with boys from a neighbouring school, the police taking the view that this was a problem which the schools should resolve themselves, the head teachers believing that the problem was serious enough to demand direct police intervention. Another head teacher wrote to his education authority to complain of persistent violent and intimidating behaviour around his school by two young people who were attending Freagarrach at the time. There is good research evidence that supports the stance of the police and Reporters on diversion: schools which try to manage their own conflicts are likely to be more effective in controlling delinquency than those which rely on outside agencies for conflict resolution (Rutter et al., 1979; Mortimore et al., 1988). Nevertheless, these examples illustrate the tensions that were inherent in the strategy between the central formulations of principles and their implementation in practice at the front line. The fact that there were few instances of this kind is a tribute to the way in which, on the whole, commitment to the strategy was maintained at the level of practice as well as that of policy.

The Young Offenders Strategy Group, then chaired by the Director of Social Work for Falkirk, and consisting of senior managers from the Education and Social Work Departments of the three local authorities, the three Reporters, senior staff from Central Scotland Police, and senior managers from Barnardo's and Apex, produced a revised *Young Offenders Strategy* in June 1998 (Central Scotland Police et al., 1998), signed by the Chief Executives of the three local authorities, the Chief Constable, the Regional Reporter, and the Director of Barnardo's Scotland. The document was formally approved by the three local authorities in the autumn of 1998. The principles of partnership between the police, local authorities and the voluntary sector which underpinned the original strategy of 1994 were strongly reaffirmed, and the document listed a number of achievements as well aspects of the original strategy where progress was made but not sustained. The achievements included the continued secondment to the Reporter's office of the Education Liaison Officer from Falkirk, the development of school-based policies against exclusion and bullying, a reduced reliance on secure accommodation for young people who offend, and a warning system for first-time offenders which had reduced referrals to the Reporter's Service. And two achievements were directly related to Freagarrach: its contribution to a 'significant' reduction in persistent offending, and its use of the TRACE database. The two areas where early progress was not sustained were the provision of access to TRACE to the Reporter's Service, and the development of a database on resources for young people (which it was originally intended should be accessible to all agencies).

The revised strategy identified areas for future work and the need to incorporate them into an action plan. These included improving data collection and information exchange across agency boundaries, the extension of the strategy to 16–18 year-olds, identifying links between substance misuse and offending, addressing the lack of suitable accommodation for young people, examining practice in residential establishments when 'incidents' occurred, reducing delays in the criminal justice process, raising local awareness of work with young offenders, learning from the evaluation of other projects, and addressing the long-term funding of Freagarrach 'subject to evaluation and evidence of continuing need'. Compared with the original strategy, the revised version was less centred on the need for a project like Freagarrach, but other elements of it repeated themes consistently identified over the previous five years as areas for improvement, notably the quality and availability of information, the lack of accommodation, and the need to develop services for young offenders old enough to be dealt with by the adult system. For the Young Offenders Strategy Group, it was important that the new strategy should be a genuine product of inter-agency co-operation, to reflect the changed composition of the partnership, and to secure a sense of ownership and commitment.

Interviews at the time with Freagarrach staff and the Chair of the Strategy Group suggested that the most important new elements of the strategy were its attempts to integrate services for substance misuse problems into other work with young offenders, and to develop services for 16–18 year-olds; and these remained central themes for the development of practice in the interviews held towards the end of the evaluation. A successful bid for funding for the latter was made to the Scottish Office, which also provided funds for a Barnardo's project (Matrix) aimed at 8–13 year-olds, and conceived strategically as linked to but separate from Freagarrach; its early work was evaluated by McIvor with Moodie (2002). The existence of a stable inter-agency partnership was important in the success of this bid, but in practice, inevitably, there were variations in agencies' capacity to deliver what they were committed to under the strategy. The police, with Barnardo's, were seen as the most reliable and consistent partners, particularly in their willingness to share information. Practice in education and social work was more variable, with some evidence, for example, that the policies adopted by all three Education Departments on minimising exclusions were difficult to implement consistently, and that in Social Work Departments there was a greater commitment to young offenders in specialist criminal justice teams than in children and families services.

All members of the strategic partnership agreed that it was very difficult to imagine an effective strategy that did not have a place in it for Freagarrach. In the summer of 1998 a central preoccupation for Barnardo's and the Strategy Group was the question of continued funding for the project. Negotiations with officials in the Scottish Office led to the conclusion that after March 2000 funds would essentially have to be found from the three local authorities, a frustrating but not wholly unexpected outcome. The main doubt about the continued commitment of the local authorities related at that stage to Stirling, whose contribution was proportionally smaller than that of Clackmannanshire or Falkirk. There was little doubt at this point, however, that there would be considerable pressure from the other agencies on any partner whose commitment to Freagarrach seemed to be wavering, since the project had come to be accepted as an integral and valued part of the resources available locally for young offenders: Freagarrach was seen not as an exotic import but as an integral and valued part of a locally developed strategy that commanded support from all agencies. It was a surprise to the other partners, then, when Clackmannanshire was the authority that withdrew funding from Freagarrach early in 2000. The reasons for this decision, which aroused anger and disappointment as well as surprise, and entailed the closure of Freagarrach's Alloa base from July 2000, were complex and will not be discussed in detail here. They included the sudden departure of a key 'champion' of Freagarrach from the Social Work Department (Rumgay and Cowan, 1998), anxiety about the size of the financial contribution expected from an authority as small as Clackmannanshire (its population of about 49,000 makes it the smallest in mainland Scotland), and a politically inspired determination to take an independent line, based on what were seen as local rather than regional needs. The general lesson to be drawn from the experience – which neither Barnardo's nor any of the other partner agencies foresaw or could have forestalled – is that even a partnership with a long history and apparently secure inter-agency support is vulnerable to sudden change, and requires constant care and maintenance.

To summarise and recapitulate: Freagarrach derived practical benefits from its status as the most visible part – 'the tip of the iceberg' – of a much wider strategy on young offenders. The most obvious of these was its access to the TRACE system; this allowed for a proactive approach to referrals on the project leader's part, and helped to ensure that all young people who met the criteria for acceptance at the project were at least considered for it, while also helping to avoid dilution or net-widening. The referral process, and the fact that the project provided open, individualised programmes of work, meant that it was rare for young people to have to wait for long after the referral before starting at Freagarrach. The original target – that the project would work with 40 young people each year – was based on the assumption that the average length of stay would be six months; in fact, as discussed in more detail below, the average number of young people who formally started at Freagarrach was 24 a year. This figure underestimates the number of young people who received some help from the project, since at least 15 were helped in various ways without ever being formally accepted for the Freagarrach programme; but there is no doubt that those who became engaged with the programme tended to stay for longer than had been envisaged. The main reasons for this were that many of the young people became highly dependent on Freagarrach and its micro-community of care, and had a range of personal and relational difficulties with which they were unlikely to receive help elsewhere; and the lack of adequate resources to support the process of moving on from Freagarrach was also an important factor.

That Freagarrach provided a caring and supportive environment is attested by the young people themselves, whose views are reported in Chapter 6. It is, however, difficult to express in words how the staff at Freagarrach managed to convey care and concern while also making clear to the young people that their offending was unacceptable. The style of work was suggestive of the practice of reintegrative shaming described by Braithwaite (1989) and regarded by Sampson and Laub (1993) as the key protective factor in parenting that enables young people who are objectively 'at risk' to avoid entering into criminal careers. The central message of the theory of reintegrative shaming is that to do nothing about criminal acts is likely to make things worse, but that to respond in a way that outcasts and stigmatises the perpetrator of these acts is likely to make things worse still. A response that conveys condemnation of the act while also communicating respect for and acceptance of the perpetrator stands a chance of making things better. The theory is in a sense a reworking of the traditional idea that in dealing with children and adolescents it is important to balance care and control; the project staff conceived this as essential to their practice from the beginning, and maintained a way of working that allowed them to confront and challenge offending among the young people at the project within an environment that provided security, safety, comfort, respect and care. For many of the young people, Freagarrach was the only setting in which they had ever experienced such treatment from adults; it is no wonder that they should have found it difficult to leave.

The core elements of Freagarrach's work remained constant throughout the period of the evaluation, but the staff were open to change and receptive to new influences: changes were made, but without losing a sense of continuity and commitment to basic principles. As well as making changes as a result of reflection on and evaluation of their own work, the staff had to respond to changes in the project's environment, and to the kind of events that will inevitably occur over a five-year period, such as movement of staff. Nevertheless, the sheer pressure of daily work meant that there was less scope for developments in practice, such as joint working with staff from other agencies, than the Freagarrach staff would ideally have wished. External changes were, in general, relatively predictable and therefore manageable, because inter-agency commitment to a common strategy survived largely intact over the period, and Freagarrach itself was an important influence on the strategy's evolution.

A consistent theme in the accounts Freagarrach staff gave of their work was that it was based on the findings of research on effective practice. In their methods of work, their adherence to a well defined target group, and in the intensity and duration of their contact with the young people who spent substantial periods at Freagarrach, the staff's practice was certainly in line with the main conclusions of research on 'what works' in programmes for offenders. But it was also essential to the project's style of work that programmes for the young people should be individualised rather than follow a single template: hence, among other things, the variation in the lengths of time young people spent at the project. It is also important to stress that the ways in which programmes are delivered may matter, in terms of outcomes, as much as their content (for a recent Scottish statement on this, see McNeill et al., 2005): a programme that contains all the prescribed elements for effectiveness is unlikely actually to work if it is delivered in a harsh, punitive and condemnatory manner. In contrast, the Freagarrach programmes were typically delivered in a way that conveyed the human qualities associated with success in helping people to change – acceptance, accurate empathy, and non-possessive warmth. These terms, taken from Truax and Carkhuff (1967), describe as well as any the distinctive style of work at Freagarrach.

Duration and Intensity of Contact

Freagarrach claimed to provide a programme of supervision whose intensity and duration were commensurate with the young people's risk of reoffending. As will be shown in Chapter 4, the project worked only with young people who met its stated criterion of persistence (and in many cases far exceeded it), and who were therefore, according to the well-established 'risk principle', drawn from the group of offenders most likely to benefit from intensive intervention (Andrews et al., 1986). If, in line with the original plan, all young people attending the project had had three contacts a week, each lasting about two hours, over a six-month period, they would have spent about 150 hours in direct contact with project workers, spread over about 80 days – giving an intensity and duration of contact close to that specified in legislation (for example, on community service and probation centres) as appropriate for the more persistent or serious offenders who receive community sentences.

In practice, both duration of stay and intensity of contact were much more variable than this – not surprisingly, given the commitment of the staff to tailoring the programme to the needs of the individual. Throughout the period of the evaluation, the average length of stay was considerably longer than six months, and some young people stayed for very much longer. This is the main reason why Freagarrach worked with fewer young people than had originally been intended, though, as noted above, this does not mean that substantial numbers of young people who could have benefited from the project were deprived of the opportunity to do so. Table 3.1 shows the mean length of stay for the first four years, most of the young people who started in 1999–2000 still being at the project at the time of the analysis. The table also shows the modal length of stay, since the mean figure gives a misleading picture in some cases because of very long (and short) stays by a few young people. It should be remembered in interpreting the table that the project staff remained in close contact with several young people who had officially left, while some who were officially attending were in fact seen only infrequently.

Of the young people who started in the project's first year, seven attended for over a year, and one stayed for almost 2½ years; in the second year, the mean length of stay was shorter, but again one young person stayed for almost 2½ years; in the third year, when the mean length of stay increased, one young person stayed for almost two years; and in the fourth year the longest stay (by two young people) was of 13 months. In general, younger offenders tended to stay for longer, and the tendency for the modal length of stay (the most frequent length of stay in each year) to decrease reflects the upward trend over time in the average age of young people starting at Freagarrach, as well as the efforts made by the staff, discussed above, to encourage young people to move on from the project.

Table 3.1 Mean and modal lengths of stay (in months) at Freagarrach 1995-99

	Length of stay		
Period	*Starts*	*Mean*	*Mode*
1995-96	21	11½	10
1996-97	23	8	7
1997-98	27	9½	6
1998-99	21	7½	6

The project's records of contact were examined at various stages of the evaluation to assess the intensity of work. On each occasion it was apparent that the amount of contact with young people varied enormously across cases, as did contact with family members and other professionals. The young people who generated the most work during their first weeks at Freagarrach tended to do so throughout their time there, by virtue of the complexity of problems in their background and continuing problematic behaviour. There was in general no strong indication that the amount of contact tailed off over time, as might have been expected; indeed, contact was often intensive during a young person's last weeks at Freagarrach, as the staff tried to make arrangements for moving on. It was in fact not unusual for young people who had formally left to remain in close contact with the project. The staff viewed this continued contact as a positive opportunity to undertake crisis intervention work, and thought it important that there should be scope for it: 'we won't turn them away'. This kind of continuing contact was inevitable given that Freagarrach functioned for many of the young people as a community of care (Braithwaite, 1995).

The type of work done with young people also varied across cases: a few young people were never involved in formal group work sessions, while others had 50 and more contacts of this kind. The number of recorded individual work sessions varied similarly, as did the amount of contact with the young people's families (from two contacts to well over 100). Some of these variations arose, of course, from the length of time young people spent at Freagarrach: nine young people who made a formal start at the project never became truly engaged with the work, and left after a few weeks (though this short period sometimes generated a great deal of activity). The principal reason for the variation is, however, that the staff were able to be flexible and adaptable, responding to assessed need (and of course to recurrent problems and crises), and trying to match their interventions to the learning styles and aptitudes of the young people. The actual workload of the project was therefore unpredictable:

in most cases there was no means of assessing accurately in advance how much time, energy and commitment a young person newly arrived at Freagarrach would require. While the project's records certainly do not record every contact with the young people or others concerned with them, they do clearly convey that the project provided intensive supervision, support and care for the great majority of young people who engaged with it all. They also convey the staff's commitment and energy: the effort and intensity of involvement with young people attending for a second time, who had characteristically gone through a chaotic period of very frequent offending before returning to the project, are especially striking. The re-acceptance of these young people is an indication of the staff's willingness to take the risk of trying to help young people whom it would have been easy to reject as having had their chance and failed to take it. Overall, there is no doubt that on average young people attending Freagarrach could expect rather more contact with project workers, over a longer period, than the original broad guideline of 75 contacts over six months implied.

In this sense, the project's practice was plainly in line with the advice of Lipsey (1995: 78) that to succeed in reducing the reoffending risk programmes need to provide 'a sufficient amount of service, preferably 100 or more contact hours, delivered at two or more contacts per week over a period of 26 weeks or more'. In addition to providing a 'dose' of the size prescribed in the effectiveness research, the project also followed both the 'risk principle' (Andrews et al., 1986) and, in its use of a variety of methods, the 'breadth principle' (Palmer, 1992). The programme focused on criminogenic needs while not neglecting others (Andrews, 1995), and, being based in the community, was more likely than an institutionally based programme to facilitate real-life learning (McIvor, 1990; McGuire, 1995). The project was adequately resourced, and staff were appropriately trained and supported (Hollin, 1995), there was a commitment to monitoring and evaluation, and activities were (in general) systematically recorded (Lipsey, 1995). These features of Freagarrach, according to available knowledge of 'what works,' should be associated with positive outcomes in terms of reoffending; and they were accompanied by a style of work that, as argued above, successfully conveyed care, empathy and warmth.

Chapter 4

The Young People at the Projects

In this chapter we consider some characteristics of the young people who attended the two projects. This is relevant to the question of whether the projects worked with their intended target groups, and to how they adapted to the characteristics of the young people they worked with. It also conveys something of the current and past problems often associated with persistent offending. Because of differences in the information collected by the projects, the same kinds of data are not always available for both.

The Young People at CueTen

Offending

The project was established to work with persistent young offenders, and although the definition of 'persistent' was kept relatively vague, a relevant measure of whether CueTen worked with the intended target group is to consider the number of charges recorded against each individual in the 12 months before referral. The figures for the young people who started from January 1996 are shown in Table 4.1, where numbers in brackets show the number of young women in each category.

Table 4.1 Number of charges in 12 months before referral, CueTen

Number of charges	Number of young people	% of young people
Fewer than 3	15 (7)	17
3–5	20	23
6–10	19 (4)	22
11–15	14	16
16–25	6 (1)	7
Over 25	12 (1)	14
Total	86 (13)	100

As can be seen, although a substantial proportion (40 per cent) of the young people had fewer than six charges, a similar proportion (37 per cent) had more than ten. The young women tended to have been charged less often, though this is not to say that they did not have (and present) difficulties comparable to the young men's. The highest number of charges recorded against an individual was 47, while another five had each accumulated more than 30. None of these six successfully completed the programme, although one did progress onto an adult job-seekers' course run by Apex.

Of the seven young women who had been charged with fewer than three offences, five were in residential or foster care, having been referred to a Children's Hearing as being beyond parental control, in need of care and protection, and/or for failure to attend school. Four of this group had not been charged in the preceding 12 months; one had only recently left residential school, but had an offending history dating back to when she was 12 years old; another had also been first charged at the age of twelve, had a very disrupted lifestyle, and was considered to be in need of some support and stability; and two had never been formally charged. Of these, both had been referred to a Children's Hearing; one was believed by her social worker to be offending, 'up to all sorts of nonsense', while the other was a chronic school-refuser, and her placement at Cue Ten resulted from a direct request from the Hearing, as an alternative to a residential requirement. Apex's policy was that the CueTen programme would be available to both males and females, and that ideally there should be a gender mix in each group; this was achieved in the first seven intakes, in the sense that each contained at least one young woman. As with other projects for persistent offenders, however, in practice the great majority (85 per cent) of young people worked with were male, and there is perhaps some indication that young women were more likely than young men to be referred to the project on 'welfare' rather than offending grounds (that is, on the basis of a judgement about their needs, not of the seriousness of their offending).

Of the remaining eight (all male) who had fewer than three charges, all but one had a history of offending, in one instance starting at the age of nine; and in most cases this was combined with referrals to a Hearing on grounds other than offending. The one young man who had not been formally charged had been referred to the Reporter on grounds of being beyond parental control and chronic truancy; he admitted offending, was described by one professional who knew him well as a 'chronic offender who is not getting caught,' and at the time of referral to CueTen was also excluded from mainstream school. Although the project was never really in a position to pick and choose which young people it would accept, all of the young people who attended can be thought of as having been appropriately (or at least not inappropriately) referred: most met the criterion of persistent offending – three offences – used by Hagell and Newburn (1994) (and, with some qualifications, in the 1994 Criminal Justice and Public Order Act in England and Wales, to establish eligibility for a Secure Training Centre). Those who did not obviously satisfy this criterion were referred to and accepted by CueTen on the grounds that they were at risk of offending and that the project had something to offer them – constructive supervision that could help in the development of social skills and the establishment of acceptable boundaries to their behaviour.

Table 4.2 shows how old the young people were when first charged (if they had been); the numbers of young women are again in brackets.

Table 4.2 Age when first charged by the police, CueTen

Age in years	Number
8	2
9	10
10	12
11	6 (1)
12	14 (4)
13	16 (1)
14	19 (5)
15	4
Not charged	3 (2)
Total	86 (13)

More than half had been charged before they became teenagers, and almost three-quarters (excluding the three against whom no charges were recorded) had been charged before their 14th birthday. About the same proportion had a record of known offending going back at least two years before they came to CueTen, since, although the project was publicised as available for 14–16 year olds, in practice it worked primarily with 15 year-olds. Seventy of the 86 young people who started at CueTen were 15 years old at the time, and most of those who were 14 were close to their 15th birthday. The lack of any training allowance meant that 16 year-olds were unlikely to be referred, even if they were still involved with the Children's Hearings System, and those who became 16 during the programme often found the lure of paid employment, normally only temporary, irresistible.

Table 4.3 Number and percentage of young people charged with different offence types, and number of charges, CueTen

Offence category	Number of young people	Number of charges
Non-sexual violence	11 (13%)	17 (2%)
Crimes of indecency	2 (2%)	3 (<1%)
Crimes of dishonesty	69 (80%)	511 (55%)
Fire raising/vandalism	46 (53%)	146 (16%)
Other crimes	10 (12%)	17 (2%)
Miscellaneous	47 (55%)	165 (18%)
Motor vehicle	20 (23%)	71 (8%)
Total	86	930

Table 4.3 shows the categories of offences with which the young people had been charged in the 12 months before starting at CueTen. It combines attempted offences with those actually committed, and shows the total number of charges in each category. The categories are those used by the Scottish Criminal Records Office.

Four-fifths of the young people had been charged with crimes of dishonesty, which also make up by far the largest single group of charges. Fire raising/vandalism and the 'Miscellaneous' category, which includes breaches of the peace and assaults, account for the bulk of the remainder. The 'Miscellaneous' category includes 85 charges of assault, over half the total charges in this category, brought against 35 young people; ten of these were also charged with non-sexual crimes of violence, so that altogether 36 of the young people who attended CueTen had been charged with violent offences of some kind. It is not surprising that the project staff had on occasions to deal with potential and actual violence. The only other significant category is offences involving motor vehicles: almost one-quarter of the young people had been charged with offences in this category, though they account for only 8 per cent of the total number of offences. The young women's offending was heavily concentrated in the 'Miscellaneous' and 'Crimes of dishonesty' categories, the miscellaneous offences being mainly minor assaults and breaches of the peace.

Problems Other than Offending

As noted in Chapter 2, a feature of working with these young people which surprised the project staff in CueTen's early stages was the extent to which their offending was just one aspect of their difficulties. This led one member of staff to remark: 'If we only had to deal with their offending this job would be quite straightforward.' As is invariably the case with a sample of persistent young offenders, many had experienced a variety of disturbances and disruptions to normal development, and endured distress and unhappiness.

Fifty-seven (66 per cent) of the young people involved with the project had previously been referred to the Reporter for issues other than offending, some several times and for several different reasons. Thirty-five had been referred on the grounds of 'failure to attend school'; the other grounds were being 'beyond parental control' and child protection issues. Thirty-six were known to have been in recent contact with other welfare professionals, mainly educational psychologists and drug counsellors, and at least 56 were considered by the CueTen staff to have a problem with drugs and/or alcohol. Others were known to have consumed these substances without this being classified as a problem, by them or anyone else.

While some of the young people used available help and advice on problems related to drug or alcohol use, others refused to consider this as an issue; and some at least considered these forbidden pleasures to be a natural part of growing up: events such as 'rolling my first joint' were milestones in their development to adulthood. Behavioural difficulties at CueTen resulting from drug or alcohol use seemed to become more marked as time went on: some young people were under the influence of drugs or alcohol, or both, almost every day, and this could lead directly to their suspension or exclusion from the project. Others were sometimes too hungover to participate in any activities. Although only seven young people had previously been charged with offences directly relating to the misuse of drugs, comments made during interviews suggested that some of the 511 offences of dishonesty were motivated by the desire to obtain money for drugs or alcohol, and that a similarly unknown number of the offences in the previous 12 months had been committed while the young people were under the influence of one or the other, or of both: 'It was only because I was steaming ....' , or 'We'd been buzzing gas ....' . Some professionals working in the area thought that the pattern of drug and alcohol use at CueTen was not peculiar to this group of young people, but merely reflected the more general use of these substances in the wider teenage community. There is no doubt, however, that this aspect of the young people's behaviour created serious problems of management for the CueTen staff, as well as limiting the young people's ability to learn from their time at the project; and the frequency of reported use by some young people suggested an emerging problem of dependency.

Family stress

If persistent offending can be seen as, in the words of a Fife social worker, a 'distress call', another element of the distress of young people at CueTen was disruption of their family life. More than three-quarters (70) had suffered some degree of family dislocation, and were not living with both their natural parents at the time of referral. For at least three of these the disruption arose from the death of a parent, and a further two were known to have experienced the loss of a sibling. Well over half the group (50) had at some time experienced care outside the family home, in most cases formal residential care; for some this had been only short-term, for purposes of assessment, but others had spent long periods away from home, and some had been in secure accommodation. Even compared with the findings of other studies of known offenders, which invariably report much higher levels of experience of local authority care than in the overall population, the figure for the young people at CueTen is strikingly high (Dodd and Hunter, 1992; Stewart and Stewart, 1993). Although most of the young people had been born and brought up in Fife, a few had also experienced the disruption caused by moving home over long distances, particularly from England. They then had to cope with the problems of settling in a new location and in a different education system, and of learning a new and very different accent. Even in the minority of cases where the family unit was on the surface reasonably stable, it could not be assumed that the young people's experience was one of safety or security. A number of them were known to have experienced violence in the home, linked in some cases to alcohol abuse. From the information available it appeared that well over a quarter (26) of the young people were living in home circumstances where violence was a real threat in their daily lives, during the time when they were expected to commit themselves to the programme offered at CueTen.

Health

Another set of problems which appears to be common among persistent young offenders, but is rarely given much attention in the literature, is associated with health or the lack of it. At least 18 of the young people at CueTen were known to have health problems which in some instances had, and would go on having, a direct bearing on the type of work they were able to undertake, or the settings in which they could do it. Asthma, eczema and psoriasis were the most common ailments, and they prevented the young people affected from working, for example, in a garage (because of the risks of exposure to oil, grease, and so on), and from taking up a college place which would have entailed prolonged contact with hairdressing products. Apart from the practical difficulties they entailed, some of these conditions were disfiguring, even if only temporarily, and likely to have a negative effect on the young people's self-esteem. Had it not been for the immediate impact of these ailments on the range of work and training opportunities available to the young people it is possible that their health problems would have escaped notice; the only study we could find which systematically sought information on the general health (as opposed to the mental health) of a sample of offenders is Stewart and Stewart's (1993) survey of young adult offenders, which found that almost a quarter of 17–23 year-olds known to the probation service suffered from some disability or an incapacitating chronic illness. It may be significant, too, that the conditions that were most common among young people attending CueTen, while physical in origin, are liable to be exacerbated by emotional stress.

Education

Of the 86 young people who attended the project, 35 had been referred to the Children's Hearing on the grounds of their failure to attend school, 26 were recorded as 'excluded' from mainstream school at the time of referral, and others had previously been excluded from school and/or transferred from one school to another because of behavioural problems. Even with a generous interpretation of what might count as 'attending school', no more than twenty of the 86 could be said to have been actually at school at the time of their referral to CueTen. In an effort to keep some of the disaffected young people in contact with the school system, the Education Department arranged flexible learning packages, involving both off-site support centres and school-based support units. In many instances full-time attendance was not thought a realistic goal, and attendance could be required for as little as one hour a day. Some of the 20 counted as 'attending' were doing so reluctantly, having already been referred for non-attendance or excluded, or both; and 12 were at a residential school, on a part-time basis in some cases, so that non-attendance was less of an option.

It is clear that more than three-quarters of the young people who came to CueTen had not been attending any educational establishment on a regular basis, or at all. For most this was a well established pattern; and, as with disruption of family life, it is a pattern that emerges strongly in surveys of delinquent populations (Devlin, 1995). The lack in so many cases of any recent habit of attending school, let alone of any positive experience of education, was undoubtedly a major factor in the problems of attendance and commitment which constantly confronted the CueTen staff, although in a few cases what CueTen offered was enough to make a positive difference, as discussed in Chapter 2. Although a small number of the young people interviewed claimed never to have liked or enjoyed school, most said that the difficulties began when they started their secondary education. Some claimed that the work was too difficult, or that they could not see any purpose in learning certain subjects. Others said that they were confused by the lay-out of the school and the requirement to move around the building between classes; this provided opportunities, which perhaps began as accidents, to 'go missing'. Many attributed their difficulties to the attitude of the teachers: those who are seen as rejecting school are liable to be rejected in turn.

It is not surprising that a project that required attendance over a 26-week period, thus removing the young person from the school system during what is supposed to be a crucial period in their education, should have received so many referrals of young people who were achieving little at school, if they were attending at all. The project was certainly seen by some social workers as providing an important resource not so much for the persistent offender, but for the less serious offender who also had school-based problems. There is no doubt, however, that with very few exceptions the young people who started at CueTen were persistent offenders, by the criteria used in Fife and elsewhere, and in most cases they had already acquired a substantial criminal career by the time they came to CueTen. The problems that they brought with them were characteristic of the general population of persistent young offenders, although a higher proportion than has been found in other studies had some experience of local authority care, whether as a result of local social work practice or of a higher than usual incidence of problems in family relationships. These characteristics inevitably had implications for the kind of work that the staff were able to do, and the way they were able to do it.

The Young People at Freagarrach

Freagarrach dealt with a wider age range of young people than CueTen, but the two groups shared many characteristics. Like the CueTen group, the young people who came to Freagarrach, predominantly young men, typically had a range of problems apart from (though no doubt often related to) their offending. These include experiences of adverse family environments, rejection of (and by) the education system, and heavy use of alcohol and other drugs.

Table 4.4 shows the age of the young people at the time of their arrival at Freagarrach, and the numbers of males and females among the 106 young people who started during the period of evaluation.

Table 4.4 Young people at Freagarrach: age and gender

				Age			
Gender	12	13	14	15	16	17	Total
Male	5	7	26	35	14	7	94
Female	0	0	1	6	2	3	12

The great majority (89 per cent) of these persistent offenders were male, as is to be expected: while young women routinely commit minor offences, serious and persistent offending is an almost exclusively male preserve, among juveniles as among adults (Graham and Bowling, 1995). Over the years the average age of young people starting at Freagarrach tended to increase: from an average of just over 14½ in the first 12 months it rose steadily to 15 and 4 months in the third year, and then to 16 in the fourth year; while the fifth year saw a drop to 15½, the overall trend was clear. Since Freagarrach at all stages accepted most of the truly persistent juvenile offenders in central Scotland, the change in the average age presents something of a puzzle: there is no logical reason to suppose that the most persistent offenders were older in 1999 than they were in 1995. In fact, TRACE data suggest that the number of known 15-year-old offenders did exceed the number of 14 year-olds in 1997 and 1998, though not in 1999; the project's intake therefore mirrored the age distribution of known persistent juvenile offenders quite closely. It was also suggested, however, that in the first year, when it was important to establish the project's credibility and demonstrate its usefulness, the staff felt some pressure to accept younger offenders who, later on, might have been diverted into other resources, or offered the kind of informal work described in Chapter 3.

Offending

Table 4.5 uses Scottish Criminal Records Office data to show the ages at which the young people were first charged with a criminal offence, counting only the 95 young people for whom at least 6 months' follow-up data are available from the time they began attending Freagarrach. It shows that two-thirds of the young people had been charged with some offence by the age of twelve – not a surprising finding given the persistent nature of the group's offending, since an early start to an offending career is a good predictor of persistence, but a slightly higher figure than for the CueTen group.

Table 4.5 Young people at Freagarrach: age at first charge

Age when first charged	Number of young people
8	14
9	8
10	11
11	12
12	18
13	12
14	10
15	5
16	7
Total	95

Table 4.6 groups the same 95 young people by the number of charges or convictions recorded against them in the year before they began attending Freagarrach. The table is again drawn not from the TRACE system but from Scottish Criminal Records; for young people who had reached the age of 16 when they started at the project this was the only source available, so the table gives an underestimate of the number of offences which led to a charge in the relevant period. The pattern is, however, similar to that shown in Table 4.1 for the CueTen group.

Table 4.6 Number of charges or convictions in 12-month period before starting at Freagarrach

Number of charges or convictions	Number of young people
1–5	29
6–10	28
11–20	28
21–30	7
31 +	3
Total	95

When the TRACE data were examined no significant change over time was found in the average number of charges recorded against the young people who attended the project. An analysis at the mid-point of the evaluation, when TRACE data were available on almost all the young people, showed an average of 17.7 charges in the 12 months before the young people started at Freagarrach. Table 4.7 shows the percentage of the total number of charges which fell into different offence categories, and the percentage of young people who had committed each type of offence. An analysis was also undertaken of the number of charges made against the young people in respect of each type of offence. Typically, young people who had been charged with any offence of dishonesty had been charged with about nine such offences; for miscellaneous offences and fire-raising and vandalism there were on average about four charges, for violence there were on average three, and for 'other' offences two. These figures give an indication both of the versatility of the young people's offending and of the types of crime and victimisation that would be prevented if it were the case that the project had a positive impact on young people's offending.

Table 4.7 Types of offence and extent of young people's involvement (12-month period before starting at Freagarrach)

Offence type	*% of total charges*	*% of young people charged with this type of offence*
Non-sexual crimes of violence	12	70
Crimes of indecency	< 1	5
Crimes of dishonesty	47	95
Fire raising/vandalism	17	73
Other crimes	3	27
Miscellaneous offences	21	86
	N = 991	N = 95

One conclusion to be drawn from this table is that the young people who attended Freagarrach were quite versatile offenders. Almost all had been charged with offences of dishonesty; as with the other offence categories, this covers a wide spectrum of offences, from the relatively minor, such as shoplifting low value goods, to housebreaking. Similarly, the 'violence' category covers everything from relatively minor assaults to (in one case) attempted murder, but most charges were at the less serious end of the continuum. The same is true of the charges of fire raising and vandalism. 'Miscellaneous' charges were mostly related to public order incidents, sometimes involving assaults, and often associated with alcohol or drug use; charges in the 'other' category usually involved drugs or the possession of offensive weapons. It is worth noting that although most of the charges of violence were for relatively minor offences, the level of involvement in violent offending was high among the Freagarrach group: both the percentage of young people charged with violent offences, and the percentage of the total number of charges which were for violence, are much higher than in the CueTen group.

Problems Other than Offending

Education

Predictably, since delinquency is strongly associated with not liking school, poor school performance, weak attachments to school and teachers, and low educational aspirations (Braithwaite, 1989), many of the young people who attended Freagarrach, like those who attended CueTen, had negative experiences of the school system. Fifty-five (52 per cent) of the 106 young people were recorded as being excluded from school at the time of starting at Freagarrach, and others had been excluded in the past; many of those currently excluded had been excluded more than once. Eighty-one (76 per cent) were known to have a history of truancy from school, and 72 (68 per cent) were adjudged to have a poor school record and to have had educational difficulties. Only 14 young people (18 per cent) out of the 80 who should have been attending school at the time they came to Freagarrach were recorded as being in mainstream education (without truancy or exclusion) at the time, an even lower proportion than at CueTen. Twenty-three were receiving some form of special educational provision, through a day unit or home tutoring, and a further six were being educated in a residential setting. The school-related problems of many of these young people were long-standing, dating back to their experiences of primary school; the move to secondary school had only exacerbated them.

Family stress

Many of the young people at Freagarrach lived in unhappy and disrupted family circumstances – again, an almost invariable finding in studies of populations of persistent offenders. Even the Freagarrach staff, however, were surprised by the frequency of experiences of serious loss or rejection in these young people's lives; they estimated that almost 90 per cent had had at least one experience of this kind, and, although there is room for argument over definitions, this figure seems broadly accurate (and is similar to that found by Boswell (1998) in her studies of juveniles convicted of serious offences in England and Wales). Ten of the young people had experienced the death of a parent or other close relative; accidents and suicide were causes of death, as well as illness. Another 19 had had to live with a close relative's severe or long-term illness, physical or mental. At least 28 young people had been rejected by one or both of their parents or immediate carers, or literally abandoned. Sixty-two had experienced the divorce or separation of their parents, and 30 had experienced some other kind of loss, such as loss of status in a step-family, continual changes of partner on the part of one of their parents, and continual changes of residence. Overall, the family background of these young people was reasonably stable and peaceful (at least on the surface) in at most 20 per cent of cases; even in these cases, the young people were likely to be described as 'out of control' by family members or social workers, at the time of their referral to Freagarrach.

Of the young people who came to Freagarrach, a quarter (26) were in some form of care when they arrived: 15 were in children's homes, five were in foster care (part-time in one case), and five were in secure accommodation or a residential school. Another eight were described as 'homeless' or were in insecure and short-term accommodation (hostels or bed and breakfast establishments). Overall, at least a third (records were not complete in all cases) of these young people had some experience of care, and it is likely that the figure (similar to that found by Dodd and Hunter (1992) among young prisoners in England and Wales) would have been higher but for the existence of Freagarrach.

Over half of the families were known to social workers for reasons other than the young person's offending, usually for child protection issues and family violence. Where parents had separated or divorced they had often gone on to form new relationships, their new partners often bringing children from their own previous relationships into the family home, with consequent potential for confusion and conflict. Other problems in parental behaviour were indicated in just under half of the young people's histories: the most frequent problems were associated with violence, alcohol or drug abuse, and mental health difficulties. Around one-third of the young people were known to have delinquent siblings, but this is probably an under-estimate, since records were not always complete. The Freagarrach staff regarded such problems in family life as closely related to the young people's involvement in offending, and sought to improve their circumstances through parents' groups and direct work with families. As noted above, direct work with families was seen as especially important with the younger end of the age range; these young people had no alternative, apart from institutional care, to continuing to live with their families. With the older age group with whom the project increasingly worked, the main task could be to help the young person come to terms with the reality of a chronically dysfunctional family experience and with the feelings of sorrow, regret and loss this entailed, and to move on to independent living. The lack of suitable resources, especially in safe and affordable accommodation, was an obstacle to the successful adaptation of these young people to life as young adults, and a major source of the work of the project with young people who had formally left.

Personal difficulties

The young people's adverse experiences of the education system and the turmoil and unhappiness that often characterised their family relationships had effects on their values, attitudes, personalities and social skills – on their ability to cope with the demands of everyday life without resorting to crime. The most obvious manifestation of difficulties in coping was the frequency of problems related to drug and alcohol use. These were formally noted in social work records and the project's referral documents in only about half the cases in which they were identified by project workers on the basis of their direct experience of the young people. Using figures from the project's records suggests that two-thirds of the young people had some problems related to misuse of both drugs and alcohol, about 10 per cent had problems related to alcohol alone, and about 17 per cent had problems related to drugs alone. Of course, it is always relevant to ask who defines drug use as problematic, and, as we suggest in Chapter 6, some young people seem to have used cannabis as part of a way of life that might be seen as preferable to the more traditional option of heavy drinking; but, judging by the case records, only seven young people (6 per cent of the total) had never been assessed by anyone as having some problem associated with substance use.

Such a high prevalence of drug- and alcohol-related problems is, once again, not surprising given the nature of the group who attended Freagarrach, but it inevitably created additional difficulties for the staff, both in terms of the immediate behaviour of the young people and of the prospects of diverting them from a criminal career. While the link between drug (and alcohol) use and criminal activity is complex (Hough, 1996), and both can be seen as elements of a way of life characterised by the pursuit of quick gratification and risk-taking, there is no doubt that for some people dependence on heroin in particular can require a level of involvement in acquisitive crime that is much higher than it would be in the absence of the need for an expensive drug. The evaluation produced some evidence that heroin use became more widespread in central Scotland during the years 1995–2000, although it was also argued that compared with some parts of Strathclyde the problem remained of manageable proportions. In relation to alcohol, while the link with crime is again complex, and it would be wrong to claim that alcohol consumption causes violent crime, there is evidence that young people who have been drinking heavily are more likely to commit, and be victims of, offences of violence, and that alcohol use can facilitate violent responses to perceived challenges and threats, especially in young men who lack self-esteem (South, 2002).

Less obvious and less well defined problems of coping were also common among the young people at Freagarrach. Many of the young people had difficulty in managing anger and aggression, a problem which could be associated with a wider lack of social and relationship skills. A few young people appeared, worryingly, to lack normal means of expressing emotion, including the emotion of remorse. In other cases, the Freagarrach staff believed that young people were being sexually exploited, an experience sometimes associated with sexual obsession or deviance on the young person's part. At a less individual level, young people were often influenced by local networks of criminality and drug-dealing: some came from families in which such behaviour was apparently accepted, others made links with such families, and others formed friendships or sexual relationships with young people who had attended Freagarrach. The staff were disposed to take as positive a view as possible of the young people with whom they worked, as described in Chapter 3; but they were at the same time clear about the reality of the problems many of the young people had in managing emotions and relationships, often as a result of their experience of deprivation and abuse.

There is no doubt that the young people with whom Freagarrach worked were, as well as being some of the most persistent juvenile offenders in central Scotland, among the most emotionally scarred and vulnerable in their age group. The style of work the staff adopted and maintained, which, as described in Chapter 3, combined the expression of care and concern with the message that criminal and anti-social behaviour was unacceptable, was probably the only means of engaging such young people, with their experiences of rejection by, and consequent suspicions of, the law-abiding adult world. Given that the young people had all the difficulties described above, there were perhaps surprisingly few problems of management and control at Freagarrach, a tribute to the skill and commitment of the staff. In considering the outcomes for these young people after they had left Freagarrach, offending is obviously an important measure of the project's impact, and this was recognised by Freagarrach staff and by staff in other agencies who knew the project well. They stressed, however, that the difficulties these young people had apart from their offending were also important, both in interpreting figures on reconvictions and subsequent charges and as a basis for measuring changes associated with problems in family life, substance misuse, educational failure, housing, and overall coping with society's demands. Such changes are less directly quantifiable than offending measures, but could be equally important in assessing Freagarrach's success or failure.

Conclusions

Both projects worked largely with their intended target group of persistent juvenile offenders, and in neither case was there evidence that any substantial numbers of young people who should have been referred to the projects were not referred, or were referred and not accepted. This was harder to establish for CueTen than for Freagarrach, whose access to the TRACE system provided a ready means of ensuring that no potentially suitable young people were ignored; but for CueTen too, when the police checked for the purposes of the evaluation, they detected few young people who met the criterion of persistent offending and were not excluded from consideration for other reasons, such as being in residential care. Both projects, therefore, dealt almost exclusively with young people who were not only persistent offenders but had often committed serious offences, and had personal and social difficulties and troubles beyond their offending. Experiences of abuse, deprivation, violence and loss have been found to be common in all studies of populations of persistent young offenders, and it is inevitable that such experiences should be reflected in attitudes, emotions and behaviour that presented the project staff with the constant challenge of how to keep the young people engaged in work of a kind that might produce helpful change.

The staff at Freagarrach were better able than those at CueTen to respond positively to this challenge, by virtue of the project's closer links with other agencies, its widely understood position as the most public manifestation of a strategy that also informed other aspects of agencies' work, and the skills and experience of the project workers themselves. In contrast, CueTen faced a continual struggle for acceptance, as described in more detail in the next chapter, and its workers had constantly to modify the rational, cognitive, educational style of work which Apex had used successfully with older offenders in their efforts to make sense to the young, troubled and often disruptive young people who were referred to the project. The CueTen staff had to learn on the job, and the three years of the project's life was hardly enough for all the lessons from practice to be fully understood and assimilated. Given the persistent and gruelling difficulties they faced, it is to the staff's credit that they stuck as closely as they did to the original criteria for acceptance at the project, long after they had come to appreciate what problems these entailed for their own practice.

Chapter 5

Perceptions and Expectations of the Projects

The importance of context for understanding the success or failure of specialist projects like CueTen and Freagarrach has already been stressed; in this chapter we try to illustrate and reinforce this point by giving more detail on the perceptions and expectations of the projects held by members of other agencies and the young people themselves. Pawson and Tilley (1997) are among those who have argued that social programmes of any kind cannot be understood without attention to the context in which they are implemented, and CueTen and Freagarrach provide striking examples of why this is so. 'Context' here includes the attitudes of staff in other agencies and the projects' interactions with them, and more internal features of the projects, such as the workers' access to organisational support, and the skills and resources available to them.

Perceptions of CueTen

The role of social workers in referring young people to CueTen was crucial. The original idea was that social workers from the local area teams would make the referrals, subject to later ratification by the Children's Hearing, and apart from the brief period in which schools made referrals directly this was the system that operated. The social workers who made the referrals inevitably did so with differing hopes and expectations. For some, the referral was a last resort effort, something to be tried when everything else had failed: 'I have only used it as a last resort, as nothing else available. I didn't expect him to show any real commitment, and he hasn't.'

Low expectations on the part of the social worker are likely to have been transmitted to the young people, further reducing the prospects of success. Some social workers, however, thought that a referral should be based on something more than desperation, and tried to be more discriminating in their decisions on whom to refer:

> I wouldn't refer anyone who is so disrupted and disruptive that there is very little likelihood of them succeeding or at least getting some benefit.

> The very troublesome pest who is persistently bothering the local community is probably more likely to benefit from what CueTen have to offer than the embittered persistent offender.

This last judgement is certainly plausible, but relies on a distinction that might not always be easy to make, and, if rigorously implemented, would exclude some of the young people for whom CueTen had been designed.

The importance attached to attendance, both in terms of regularity and duration, varied among social workers. Some felt that the project could be most useful in helping the young people through a specific stage in their lives, and that attendance for the whole 26 weeks of the programme, while desirable, might not be essential:

> What they get out of the project overall is more important than strict enforced attendance.

> If they decide they aren't going to attend then so be it, we just have to accept it, that they don't see it as relevant to them at that point.

Again, this is not exactly the kind of message that the CueTen staff hoped the young people would receive; but the dominant view among social workers was that these young people could not be forced to do things they were not willing to do. Sometimes this led them to explicitly modest hopes and expectations about what CueTen could achieve:

> It isn't going to have much influence on many... it is effectively a short-term containing facility, but a necessary one for that group at that point in time.

CueTen, of course, was conceived as a great deal more than a containing facility that might, for a time, encourage young people into constructive activities and leave them with less time available for offending; and the project staff naturally felt that such limited ambitions were unhelpful. They were trying to convey the importance of full attendance and participation, but without much support from social workers.

Certainly, there were other social workers who talked more optimistically: of the young people learning to behave and interact within a group and within set boundaries, of their being encouraged to feel that their input was valued, and of their learning about the process of gaining employment:

> This provides a structure, a routine to life, can help build up confidence and social skills; they hadn't enjoyed school, but can get an enjoyable positive experience while being prepared for the adult world of work.

And occasionally social workers reported that young people 'stuck at' CueTen against their expectations.

Several social workers, however, criticised the assumptions on which CueTen was based. The original target of 32 persistent young offenders a year was seen as over-ambitious, and the requirement that they go to a Children's Hearing to be made subject to a supervision order as unnecessary and even potentially damaging. There were not enough serious offenders to produce a large number of appropriate referrals, and it was better that the larger number of persistent, but not serious, offenders should be kept out of the official system and worked with on a voluntary basis:

Going to a panel can definitely be an issue; we would never put someone into the system to get them into CueTen. We do manage to keep some out, as panel members and Reporters know the work we are doing, and so a supervision order is superfluous as the work carries on regardless.

Some social workers were reluctant to recommend to a Hearing that attendance at CueTen should be required even when the young person had already been involved in the system. They feared the possible consequences if the placement did not work out and the case had to be returned to the Hearing as a failure, leading to the possibility of more intrusive measures of intervention than would otherwise have been thought necessary. While formally there is no penal tariff within the Children's Hearings System, in practice social workers tended to believe that disposals were likely to become more severe in the course of an offending career. Even a system as welfare-orientated as the CHS thus seemed to some workers more likely to do harm (through negative labelling) than good (through conveying appropriate moral messages or making helpful resources available) – the position adopted by many juvenile justice workers in England and Wales during the 1980s, that widening the net (or thinning the mesh, in Cohen's (1985) metaphor) of formal social control is always to be resisted (Smith, 1995). CueTen's association with the formal system of the CHS made it suspect, although the measures available in the CHS are nothing like as punitive as those of the youth justice system south of the border, and in fact there was little evidence during the evaluation that failure at CueTen led to an escalation of sanctions through the CHS.

Their preference for informal, voluntary work with young people led some social workers to the view that it would be better if they could work in a more flexible, collaborative way with CueTen; they felt that the chances of success would be greater if attendance were voluntary and the young person did not feel a need to rebel against imposed authority, and that voluntary attendance would allow the development of more flexible and creative 'packages' of work. Interviews with the young people themselves suggested, however, that for many it was the element of compulsion that got them to attend in the first instance, even though this effect did not always prove durable. While voluntary attendance, with appropriate encouragement from social workers and perhaps from parents, might have produced fewer problems of resentment and disruption, it is hard to believe that more than a few young people would have come regularly to the project on a voluntary basis; the CueTen programme, however flexible staff tried to make it, was simply not designed to accommodate young people who might drop in when they felt a need for support or advice – and of course the project was located a long way from the homes of most of the young people who attended it.

It might have been expected that over the life of the project social workers would become more familiar with its aims and style of work, that mutual understanding would develop, and that this would lead to more, and more appropriate, referrals. While for some social workers CueTen did become an accepted feature of the local scene, problems persisted in the quality of information CueTen received from social workers. Few social workers became reliable allies of the project, in part because of a high level of change and movement in the Social Work Department: the 86 young people who started at CueTen came from referrals by more than 50 social workers. Some social workers believed that the CueTen staff expected too much of the young people, particularly in terms of their commitment to work. Others commented that they had sometimes felt a certain inconsistency in decisions taken at the project: for no obvious reason, some young people appeared to get a number of supposedly 'final' warnings, while others were excluded more quickly. Some suggested that they should have been more involved with the decision to exclude, instead of just being told that it had been made. On the other hand, the CueTen staff sometimes found it very difficult to get social workers to attend meetings to discuss the kind of problems which might lead to exclusion, which in the nature of things often had to be called at short notice.

Social workers who articulated a clear position on CueTen usually argued that the need met by the project was quite age-specific, a view shared by providers of education and training, and by the young people themselves. For them, CueTen was of its nature a post-school resource, helpful as part of young people's transition to the adult world, since it gave an opportunity to those still of compulsory school age, though not attending, to focus on the next phase of their lives and begin to understand the world of work. The natural progression from CueTen was therefore into employment, training, or a college placement: a return to school could be seen as a step backwards, both by the young people and their social workers. This view may also have been that of Children's Panel members. The one known instance where a Children's Panel did not agree with the social worker's recommendation of a requirement to attend CueTen involved a boy who had just reached the age of 14. The Panel members apparently thought that it would be too difficult for him to be reintegrated into school after a period at CueTen, and instead requested residential care. The CueTen staff themselves continued to believe that the project could deal effectively with the younger age group, in an environment where there was perhaps less pressure than at school and where the young people did not 'stand out' as they would at school, but there were in practice few cases of successful reintegration to mainstream schooling. There is little doubt that the value of CueTen was inherently that it could help with the achievement of the transition towards greater independence and adult – or almost adult – status.

Inter-agency Communication

Chapter 1 considered the circumstances in Fife at the time when CueTen was established, and the history of problematic inter-agency communication described there had direct and lasting effects on the project's work; in particular, the provision of relevant information to the project was an issue throughout its life. The project staff themselves, again reflecting Apex's general style and lack of experience with a younger age group, did not originally realise the importance of having full information on the young people at the time of referral. They assumed that they would be given all relevant details at the outset, and be kept informed of changes in the young people's circumstances, in the same way as they gave weekly reports to social workers or schools on the progress of the young people at CueTen. This was not the case, and the project staff often had to seek additional information, even after modifying the referral and initial information forms to cover (as far as possible) all relevant issues. Although no one explicitly said that as a voluntary sector organisation, and one with a novel and untested approach, CueTen should not receive comprehensive information, and despite the official view of social work managers that it should, the project staff felt at times that relevant information was withheld. For example, when CueTen staff sent out forms requesting additional information from social workers, and the forms were not returned, or returned not fully completed, the staff sometimes felt that this was indicative of the way they were viewed by the 'professionals' – as marginal to their main concerns, and not deserving a high priority as social workers managed their heavy workloads.

Social workers' practice varied, of course, and some gave as much information as the CueTen staff asked for; but there were others who, the project staff knew, would not be so forthcoming. The apparent unwillingness on the part of some social workers to involve the project fully sometimes extended beyond the initial stage of referral and information-gathering: fundamental developments could take place in a young person's life, such as changes in household composition or even a move to another address, about which the project staff found out only by chance, from the driver who brought the young people to CueTen, or from another member of the group. Requests to be kept informed about changes in the circumstances of young people in local authority care were sometimes ignored, so that the staff found themselves confronted by troubled or troublesome behaviour without having any idea of possible reasons for it. Such problems of communication are certainly not unique to CueTen; they are always liable to arise when a specialised project relies for its referrals on other agencies. They are, however, more likely if the referring agents see the project as a dumping-ground for their most intractable cases, or if they have an agenda of their own and a view of the project's purposes which is not wholly compatible with the project's own perceptions. As we have seen, this was the case with some, though certainly not all, of the social workers who referred young people to CueTen. The project's experience in this respect highlights the need for attention to be given from the first stages of project planning to structures of communication and support in the network of agencies within which projects have to work, a point somewhat neglected in research on the effectiveness of community-based programmes for offenders (Braithwaite, 1993).

Information from the police was also a problematic issue throughout the project's life. As was noted in Chapter 1, the police were not really included in the discussions which led to the establishment of CueTen, and although the project staff asked for details of young people's offending histories from the first months of the project, these were not forthcoming, and the problem was only taken up by Apex at a senior level in the third year of the project's work. It was perhaps another sign of Apex's inexperience in working with young people that systematic information on offending careers was not sought from the outset as part of the referral process, but staff quickly realised that without this knowledge their ability to plan relevant counselling and training sessions was limited. All they had to go on was whatever information the social worker had given at the time of the referral, and the young person's own, not necessarily reliable, version of events. Late in the project's life talks began between

Apex management and the police about the feasibility of keeping the CueTen staff up to date with the young people's offending pattern during their time at the project, but nothing was agreed, and the staff continued to rely on what information they were able to glean from other sources.

Another possible symptom of the erratic state of inter-agency communication, and of the pressures that followed local government reorganisation, was that although staff in the Social Work Department and elsewhere had always intended to set up a local advisory group for the CueTen project this was not actually done until the project had been running for over a year: the group first met in March 1997. The impetus came from the Service Manager (Children and Families) in the Social Work Department rather than from Apex, whose senior staff tended to be sceptical of the value of such bodies, and it was he who chaired the group. Its members included representatives of the Reporter's Department, the police, social work (in addition to the chair), Glenrothes College, the Education Department, and a member of the Children's Panel. A representative of local employers was invited, but attended only one meeting, as did a representative of the young people at the project; neither group, therefore, had a voice in subsequent discussions. The advisory group was a setting in which problems of communication and information flow such as those discussed above could be explored, along with the recurring question of how to attract more referrals; but the group lacked executive authority, and never became the kind of advocate for the project which the staff had hoped for.

The circumstances of the project's establishment, and the support or lack of support which it received from local agencies, also had an impact on the CueTen staff's perspective on the project and their commitment to it. Contrary to the practice often adopted (for example in the case of Freagarrach) in setting up special projects, CueTen had no staff who were seconded from other agencies, and their consequent sense of insecurity of employment had an inevitable destabilising effect. Even in the project's early stages staff had to consider the question of future funding and their own future employment prospects, rather than being able to concentrate without distraction on their immediate tasks and possibilities for development. These difficulties would have been largely avoided if the staff had been able to feel secure in their employment, but secondment would, of course, have required an approach to establishing a network of inter-agency support that was more measured than the one Apex in fact adopted.

Perceptions of Freagarrach

The professionals we interviewed about Freagarrach – social workers, teachers and police officers, the main front line staff involved – were overwhelmingly enthusiastic about the project, and the more they knew about it, the more enthusiastic they tended to be. As with all 'consumer' studies, it should be borne in mind that these interviews were with a self-selected group (and the same applies to the interviews with parents and young people described below): by definition, they were people who knew something of the project and were willing to give up time to talk about it. They saw it as a valuable resource and, when they had had the experience of working directly with Freagarrach staff, they were full of praise for their commitment and skills. In these cases, when the project staff were able to work with the committed support of social workers and education staff, it is certainly true, as one social work manager remarked, that it would be wrong to attribute any credit that was due to Freagarrach alone; the achievement of a good outcome should be seen as the result of a collaborative effort. But, as was shown in Chapter 3, collaboration was inherent in the conception and operation of Freagarrach.

Freagarrach was valued by other professionals – and by members of the Children's Hearing Panels – for two main reasons: its practice with young people was highly regarded, and it was seen as a catalyst that helped to ensure the continued coherence of the broader strategy. While most of those interviewed recognised its contribution in both areas, the first reason was particularly stressed by those who had actually worked with Freagarrach, and by Reporters, the police and social work staff; the second was emphasised by staff from education departments, and by the police. Those who knew the Freagarrach staff typically described them as 'very helpful, caring, and enthusiastic'. They were seen by the police as capable of having a long term impact on the young people at the project by awakening in them a 'newly developed conscience;' their skills, and the time they were able to devote to individuals, were thought to enable them to 'do better than anyone else ever could,' even on specific problems such as drug abuse. Staff were praised for their commitment and dedication, and for their efforts to involve parents in the work with young people, which were seen as successful because they were based on a commitment to partnership, rather than on a didactic approach (which the parents might have construed as blame). It was generally agreed that Freagarrach had in fact worked with the most persistent juvenile offenders in the region; no interviewee suggested otherwise.

Reporters to the Children's Hearings System spoke very positively about the project, and their view was apparently shared by panel members: 'Panel members – rave, rave, rave – would lose a tremendous amount of faith if Freagarrach wasn't there'. It was 'wonderful to have that kind of resource… other Reporters are envious', and Freagarrach was believed by Reporters to have reduced the need for residential care across the three authorities. Progress reports from Freagarrach were thought 'very, very useful' by Reporters and panel members, and the attendance at hearings, when required, of Freagarrach staff was 'tremendously helpful'. The standard of reports was 'very good – occasionally it almost tips into advocacy for the young person [which is] not necessarily a bad thing'. The progress reports and the personal accounts from staff allowed Reporters and panel members to acquire a good sense of Freagarrach's practice, which was perceived as cognitive-behavioural work of the kind supported by research, and which 'social workers can't do or don't have time for'. The faith both Reporters and panel members had in Freagarrach meant that they were willing to allow young people to remain there without being reviewed at hearings as often as would otherwise have been the case, given the seriousness of their offending. The staff's willingness to persist in work with young people after they had reached an age when they could be regarded as the responsibility of the adult criminal justice system was also noted: 'Social workers at 16½ sometimes say, "Ach, let him go". The Freagarrach staff say there needs to be the structure of a supervision order – they're still working with them'. But in most cases

> liaison between social workers and Freagarrach is very good and very positive – it must help social workers as well, because it's never just offending that's an issue. Other social work issues are for the fieldworkers to deal with.

Other interviewees, especially from social work, tried to take a more critical, detached position: 'it's seen as a Good Thing, because everybody says it is. I've started to look more critically, recently'. But even from this perspective, 'I'm not aware of any criticisms of Freagarrach's work – invariably staff are pretty positive about it':

> In terms of their actual way of working, staff and managers speak pretty highly of it. The seconded worker was taken aback to find her diary wasn't full every day – a very positive thing, that they've time to think.

Like other interviewees, this senior member of social work staff said that it was widely accepted locally that there was often 'quite a dramatic reduction in young people's offending during the period of engagement with the project'. A reduced level of offending, and of victimisation, was the measure of Freagarrach's performance most frequently cited in the interviews, though it was also recognised that its impact on offending ought not to be judged overnight.

The other value attributed to Freagarrach concerned its contribution to the maintenance of a coherent strategy and, relatedly, its impact on other parts of the juvenile justice system. Freagarrach was described as 'the catalyst or glue for our strategy', the still point in a changing environment that had enabled the retention after local government reorganisation of multi-agency and cross-council working, and therefore of economies of scale. Staff in education and the police were especially likely to say that Freagarrach, as a visible sign of commitment to a coherent strategy, had influenced thinking and practice in their agencies: 'it has had an enormous impact on the way we deliver our service' (from the police); 'it has aided in sensitising people to the needs of "difficult" young people' (from the education service). There were instances of 'good collaboration' between Freagarrach and teachers, and when collaboration was less good this was attributable to variations among schools, not to Freagarrach's failure to deliver: 'it was ahead of its time five years ago. The education service is now catching up'. There was still room, however, for Freagarrach's influence to increase, so as to promote 'long term changes in ways of working' (in education).

Freagarrach's more direct impact on other parts of the system was also mentioned by several interviewees, and was seen as relevant to judgements of its success. Few of those interviewed had a clear view of what its overall impact might have been, but one who had consciously examined the question estimated that over the five years Freagarrach had prevented the need for expensive residential accommodation for 17 young people (more than half of those it had worked with from this local authority). The question arose, for this interviewee, of whether this represented effectiveness and value for money; to answer this, it would be useful to know what effect Freagarrach had had on the overall use of residential care. Social work staff were uncertain whether Freagarrach had reduced the use of residential care; in the absence of clear evidence that it had declined over the five years, the most optimistic view was that it had probably 'kept things on a fairly even keel' – that is, prevented a major increase. The clear view among Reporters, however, was that the project's existence did reduce the demand for residential care, and this was echoed from the police perspective: 'it doesn't look expensive when you compare it with the alternatives'. This was on the assumption that Freagarrach had not only displaced care and custody in a substantial number of cases but had reduced the number of crimes and victims in central Scotland: the evidence for both claims is reviewed in Chapter 6.

The Views of the Young People and their Families

The young people from both projects who were interviewed about their time there gave positive accounts, and while this result needs to be treated with some caution because of the self-selection problem (and because in research on projects for people who offend it is always easier for researchers to contact those who have had relatively good experiences than those who have had bad ones – that is, successes are easier to talk to than failures (Calverley et al., 2004)), it suggests that despite its difficulties CueTen, as well as Freagarrach, was capable of delivering a positive experience.

At CueTen the most common reasons given by young people for feeling positive about the project were to do with how different it was from school. Interviewees repeatedly spoke of the willingness of the CueTen staff to listen to them and discuss difficulties and problems: this was 'totally not like school'; 'they don't shout at you here, they *ask* you to do things'. It was relatively rare for this positive response to lead to radical behavioural change, but when it did so the result could be impressive: one young person whose alienation from school seemed complete – 'I kept getting into trouble for bunking off, but I only had to go for two hours on a Wednesday so I didn't think it would matter' – attended CueTen daily with virtually no absences. When young people were able to make and sustain a commitment to CueTen there could be benefits in social as well as vocational learning: young people spoke of 'calming down', and learning the difference between being assertive and being aggressive. The most valuable learning of a more conventionally educational kind seemed to be in basic literacy and numeracy; here CueTen had the advantage over school that the young people were not labelled as troublesome low achievers: 'I actually enjoy coming here, like the folks for some reason. At school I stuck out, and if anything happened they blamed me'. Parents, or more accurately mothers, also welcomed the patience and concern conveyed by CueTen staff in their contacts with them, which were usually by telephone: they found CueTen staff accessible and supportive in a way that social workers, who were too busy and had too many other people to worry about, were not.

The opinions of Freagarrach the young people expressed in interviews were overwhelmingly positive, and this was far from being only because they believed (though many did) that the alternative would have been residential care or custody. Many of their comments related to the qualities they perceived in the staff, who were often contrasted favourably with social workers. A few young people discriminated among staff members, preferring some to others, or singling out individuals as especially helpful, but more often they referred to the staff group as a whole. They spoke warmly of 'the way they talked to you and the way they treated you', of how 'understanding' they were, and of how they were 'not scared to have a laugh and a joke'. Staff were described as 'pals, identical to pals', with whom it was possible to talk 'about things I wouldn't talk to anyone else about':

> The people here let you talk to them. You can have a laugh. They have helped me so that I drink less now, control my temper more. They make you think about what you are doing, although it doesn't always stop you.... The best thing about this place is the staff.

This sentiment was echoed by several young people: the staff were seen as understanding, as having time, and as prepared to 'see your point of view': 'The best thing about this place is that the staff talk to you. They listen and they understand'. Several young people contrasted their experience of the Freagarrach staff with their much more negative perceptions of social workers. Even the minority of young people who were lukewarm about the project and unable to identify specific gains from their attendance recognised that the staff treated them with respect: 'the staff here don't push it. You can talk if you want to, but you don't have to'. Staff were also praised for their persistence and patience: '[she] would nag and nag and nag – that might be why I've stopped'. 'Nagging' here is defined positively, as an indication of the staff member's willingness not to give up but to retain and convey faith in the young person's ability to grow and change. This refusal to give up was also identified by people who came to work at Freagarrach during the course of the evaluation as perhaps the 'magic ingredient' – what made the project distinctive.

The young people were asked about what they did at Freagarrach. Perhaps half of them were able to talk articulately about the work they had done: 'some of the worksheets were useful – why you did it, what you did it for'; 'the cartooning has helped. We look at crimes and find the danger path'. Some young people said that they preferred individual work, because of the discomfort they felt in talking in a group or, occasionally, because they thought that associating with other offenders would increase the risk of their reoffending; it was not unusual for young people's main experience of Freagarrach to be exclusively of an individual relationship with one worker. Other young people felt more comfortable in groups, and the project staff were able to adapt their style of work to match the preferred learning styles of the young people; the young people's responses frequently confirmed the claim of the project staff that they were working according to the principles of effectiveness research, including the principle that a substantial minimum 'dose' of intervention is required to produce an effect: typically, the young people said that they attended the project for three sessions a week. 'Cartooning' – drawing the events leading up to an offence in comic book style – was generally (but not universally) preferred to writing: indeed, anything that reminded the young people of school work tended to be disliked. The following is a rather extreme statement of this position:

> The worst things about coming here are having to do the work. We have a folder and do stuff on how do you keep out of trouble... how to say No to your pals when you go out

with them. We spend ages doing that, at least 45 minutes. It's just like school, and I hated that about school.

This young person also believed, however, that 'this helps keep me out of trouble… They explain to me what is going to happen if I commit a crime, they make me think about it'. Of all the aspects of the Freagarrach programme, it was the visit to Glenochil that was most often mentioned as specifically helpful. This was, of course, a well defined and spectacular event, and it often proved memorable: 'the best thing I've done here is probably the Glenochil programme. We really got to see what it was like, nothing like I thought it would be. Definitely don't want to end up there'.

Young people who did not give a clear account of the work they did at Freagarrach nevertheless often believed that it was useful because at least it kept them 'off the streets', or kept them busy. The importance of structure in the lives of young people not at school or at work should not be underestimated: 'I was OK when I was here, but when I left I got bored, took too much drink and drugs and went daft. I can't do that now as I'm too busy'. Young people also often mentioned the activities they engaged in at the project, from the modest and everyday, such as playing pool, to more exciting and unusual events such as go-karting, visits to attractions such as 'Sea World at Queensferry', and outdoor activities: 'I've had the chance to do things like going on Venture Scotland, which involved a week's sailing, rock climbing, and all sorts that I wouldn't have been able to do'. To judge from the interviews, the young people generally understood that these excitements were privileges that had to be earned through work and a demonstrable change in their behaviour: 'if I keep out of trouble for two months I get to go go-karting, that's the deal, and that's the best thing about this place'. Another form of valued special event arose from Freagarrach's reputation and its commitment to informing others about its work: 'you meet all sorts of people that you wouldn't normally, like our MP'.

Behind the work and the enjoyable activities was the environment the staff created – one of safety, comfort and nurture. One young person summed up this feeling when he described the project as being 'like a wee family'. Among the benefits this family provided was the fundamental one of physical sustenance, the most basic of human needs: the frequency with which food was mentioned by the young people suggests both what Freagarrach offered and what their own families did not. The staff told the young people, 'This is *your* kitchen', and from observation as well as the interviews, they used it as their own, sometimes taking food home even though there was no suggestion that food of some kind would not be available there. One young man thought the best thing about Freagarrach was that 'we always have pizza and garlic bread'; another said:

Coming here can help me and others. You can get trouble off your mind, it can make you happy. We get food and drink – I've been taken to McDonald's. I will come here for at least six months, I will come for longer if I can.

The stress on food and comfort is a reminder of the basic deprivations endured by many of these young people, a core reality of their experience that an exclusive focus on their offending could tend to obscure. It is no wonder that some spoke of how hard it would be to leave: 'Leaving is hard, the place just grows on you'; 'this is my last day. I'm sad to be leaving but they have said that I can still contact them if I need any help'; 'I don't want to leave'.

The young people were asked what impact Freagarrach had had on them. While a very few said that there had been no impact – 'it just goes in one ear and out the other, I don't remember anything we do. That was the same at school' – most were able to identify a positive effect:

> Most of my offending was drink-related. I'm hardly ever drunk now, I do it in moderation now. It helped me look after myself a bit better, opened up opportunities about what I could do if I put my mind to it. It's been an eye-opener – having someone to talk to. Got a lot off my chest. I enjoyed going.

Other young people talked of the effect of the offending-focused work in helping them resist peer pressure, think of the consequences for themselves of offending, consider the impact on the victim, and control their anger: 'This place has calmed me down. I now know to watch my behaviour in public, to respect people and not cause grief'. Effects on their ability to cope with other aspects of their lives, less directly related to offending but still clearly linked to it, were also mentioned: 'It's been great coming here over the years. They helped me when my parents split up. I've had serious problems and they have done a lot'. One young woman spoke of the support she had had in coming out of care:

> All of Freagarrach have made it possible for me to leave the care system and settle here. If they hadn't been here to help me I think I would have cracked up – I didn't think anyone was listening to me. Now I have learnt to think before I speak, or even do anything. The work here has helped me look at why I was getting so angry and how to cope. I wouldn't have managed without this place.

The accounts of the young people confirmed what was suggested by observation and discussion with the staff: that Freagarrach worked in a way that was in line with the implications of research on effectiveness while at the same time providing an environment that was perceived as safe, accepting and caring. While a few young people were critical of some staff members, or openly sceptical about whether Freagarrach – or anything else – could have much effect on their behaviour, the great majority spoke warmly of their experiences at the project, both of their day-to-day relations with the staff (or a particular member of it) and of the work they did on offending and related issues. Many also claimed that their time at the project had enabled them to change, most often specifically in their propensity to offend, but sometimes in related areas of their lives such as controlling their temper and reducing their use of alcohol. Perhaps the most striking aspect of the interviews, however, is that for many of these young people Freagarrach was a place in which their most basic needs were met as they had not been met anywhere else. It was a micro-community of care whose closest model was that of a warm, caring family – but one in which unacceptable behaviour was signalled as unacceptable (Braithwaite, 1995).

The views of the parents and carers of the young people, as obtained from interviews, often echoed the young people's perceptions. It is likely that the parents and carers who made themselves available for interview were among those with the most positive views of Freagarrach (though some were critical of some aspects of the project), and this should again be borne in mind in interpreting the material that follows, although it is also true that in general it confirms the accounts of the young people and the findings of our observations. There were critical comments from a few parents or other carers, mostly associated with the view that the Freagarrach staff were unduly 'lenient'; but this view sometimes arose from self-serving accounts by young people of what was expected of them: 'they said I don't have to go if I don't want to', and the like. One young person's parents complained that the project paid insufficient attention to their needs as distinct from their son's, but in general parents felt that Freagarrach staff were also concerned with their interests and difficulties.

Like the majority of the young people, parents and carers praised the Freagarrach staff for their understanding, their willingness to accept young people who had been rejected by other institutions, and their accessibility. As with the CueTen mothers, these qualities were sometimes contrasted with the perceived unhelpfulness of social workers, though this did not always entail blame: parents recognised that the Freagarrach staff had far more time to devote to the young people than could be expected of a social worker: 'I think it's the time they can devote to one case'. They felt that the staff 'could get to the bottom of his problem when I couldn't', or that 'they have the ability to read the person; they seem to understand and get inside his brain quickly'. Parents often mentioned improvements in the young person's behaviour at home which they attributed to the project, and which brought benefits for them as well: 'the house was a total war zone, now it's different'; 'the whole family have gained a lot'. Their sense that the Freagarrach staff accepted the young people was expressed in terms of an ability and readiness to 'see the good side' of the young person, to treat 'kids as people', and the view that 'they give respect and therefore get it back'. One mother spoke of how the young people at the project 'had such a reputation and couldn't go anywhere, but Freagarrach accepted them'. She, like others, and like some of the young people, worried about what would happen when the time came for her son to leave: 'the only thing I feel is what happens afterwards. There's nowhere for them to go'.

Parents could regret the ending of a young person's time at the project on their own behalf too: 'I miss it, to tell the truth'. Like others who had attended the meetings for parents, this mother had found them a source of support and reassurance, after some initial anxiety: 'I felt I was the only person, but met other people with similar and worse problems'. The meetings were appreciated as social events – 'we socialised rather than questions, questions, questions' – that had a supportive purpose and effect:

I made friends with other mothers and still come to the meetings even though X [her son] has left the project. It is helpful to listen to others and realise that they have similar problems and difficulties, that their social worker is useless as well, that they have neighbours who are always complaining about kids just being kids, that the police always assume that it is their lad who has done everything that happens in the area.

Parents also usually said that they found the Freagarrach staff accessible and helpful:

> if anything was upsetting me, I would phone A or B [naming staff members]... I felt I could relax and talk to them so they gave me support. The relaxed style of the work meant that contact with the staff was informal and non-threatening; staff members would 'come in and have a chat' with the parents after driving the young person home from the project.

The impression from the interviews is that these were caring and concerned parents (usually mothers); the problems in their family relationships arose not from a lack of love and care but from uncertainty about how to express these feelings while at the same time setting and maintaining boundaries on the young person's behaviour. Freagarrach provided these parents with support and reassurance, and (in contrast to the experience several had had with social workers and others whom they had met as a result of their child's delinquency) they did not feel that the project staff reproached or condemned them for their failings or inadequacies. These were parents who wanted to work on improving their relationships with their children and were prepared to accept help to do so. Not all the parents of the young people at Freagarrach were so ready to become engaged in a co-operative process: the attitude of others towards their children's delinquency was overtly rejecting and angry, and still others had never been able to provide a safe, loving environment for their children. While there are good indications from research that projects that involve parents in their work with young offenders are likely to produce better results than those that do not (Nuttall, 1998), it is inevitable that some parents will be unable or unwilling to become involved.

Conclusions

The CueTen staff had to cope with problems which might not have arisen had the project been established more slowly, more carefully, and with more attention to local interests and sensibilities. Some basic questions, such as the kind of information the project required when a young person was referred, and its entitlement to know about continued offending and other developments in the young people's lives, were never satisfactorily resolved. These uncertainties increased staff anxiety and doubt as to how CueTen was viewed – what kind of resource it was thought to be. The match between the project's view of itself and others' views of it was not perfect. Some young people certainly came to CueTen without having received the messages about its purposes and expectations which the staff would have wished.

In contrast, Freagarrach enjoyed a high level of support within the relevant constituencies of users of the service and personnel in agencies that supported the project and were supported by it. Those with the most direct experience of Freagarrach – the young people who attended it and their families – were (judging from interview material) overwhelmingly positive about the project's work. They confirmed the conclusions reached from the observation and analysis of the process by which Freagarrach delivered its service: that this was not only in line with the findings of research on effectiveness, but characterised by the successful communication of a sense of care, respect and faith in young people's capacity to grow and change. Freagarrach accepted, in the fullest sense, young people who had been rejected by other agencies, and often by their parents; and it worked with them in a way that conveyed, 'We will not give up on you'. The staff from other agencies who were interviewed all agreed: 'we all know it's working for the kids' – and, it could be added, for many of their families. All those interviewed, but especially the police officers, were convinced that Freagarrach had had a demonstrable impact on the number of offences committed in central Scotland, and therefore on the number of victims. There was less certainty about the impact Freagarrach had on other aspects of the system, though it was widely thought that its presence and example had encouraged changes in routine practice, particularly in the police and education services. Its effect on the use of residential care was a particular issue that concerned social work staff: they saw this as a key issue when assessing costs and benefits for local authorities. This is among the issues addressed in the following chapter, and in more detail in Chapter 7, which considers benefits and costs.

Both projects emerge with credit from our interviews with the young people who attended them. With the proviso about sample bias noted above, we can concluded that the staff in both projects were able to convey interest, concern and care, in ways that the young people contrasted favourably with their experiences of school and of social work. But while the Freagarrach staff were working within an empirically tested model, and, importantly, doing so with enthusiasm and understanding within a supportive environment, the CueTen staff were engaged in a constant struggle to make sense of a model of working that was untested in the field of juvenile justice, and from the beginning proved difficult to implement with the designated target group of persistent offenders. Many young people who went to CueTen appreciated the effort and commitment of the staff, but effort and commitment were often not enough to overcome the disruptive resistance to full participation in the programme of many of those who attended. The caring, family-like experience many young people had at Freagarrach was not available at CueTen, where argument, conflict, tension and aggression were the dominant issues of daily life. The young people who attended CueTen were, for the most part, those for whom Apex had been funded to provide a service, but they were not those most likely to benefit from what CueTen had to offer. How they and the young people at Freagarrach fared during and after their time at the projects is the subject of the next chapter.

Chapter 6

The Effectiveness of the Projects

In this chapter our primary concern is with how successful the two projects were in reducing the rate of offending among the young people with whom they worked. Throughout the evaluation it was stressed by both Scottish Office (later Scottish Executive) staff and our interviewees in Fife and central Scotland that this was the crucial test, but that this did not mean that other impacts the projects might have were not important, for example on family life and relationships, educational and employment status, and general coping ability. We therefore consider outcomes other than offending, insofar as these are known, before turning to the criminal records of the young people during their time at the project and after they left. The length of the follow-up period and the quality of available data differed between the projects, so not all the findings are directly comparable, but enough are to allow for conclusions about the projects' relative success.

Employment, Education and Family Life

Information on these aspects of the young people's lives is inevitably less complete and systematic than the data on known offending, since there is no formal, centrally held record of their achievements in getting jobs or qualifications, or of their personal relationships. For the young people at CueTen, the most striking aspect of the information we have is that while failure to complete the programme was certainly associated with a higher rate of offending, both before and after attendance at the project, it was not so clearly associated with failure in other areas of personal and social development, perhaps because the meaning of non-completion of the programme is not always transparent. For example, we interviewed two young women who attended erratically for only a few weeks, but still seem to have gained something from the project. One, who said that she only went to CueTen because 'it would look good at my panel', went to Apex's adult unit for help with finding a job; the other, of whom her social worker said that 'she chooses what she will do, and will only co-operate if she sees something in it for her', had fond memories of her time at CueTen, and believed it had helped her, though she could not say how. Both these young women had been convicted of at least one offence after leaving CueTen, but when last contacted one seemed to be settling contentedly into motherhood, and the other was in full-time employment.

Even among the group of 20 young people who were excluded from CueTen because of their behaviour at the project, there was some later evidence of a maturation effect. At the time of their referral to CueTen, some of these young people were probably just not ready for what the project had to offer, and should not have been referred. The staff acknowledged this possibility by being prepared to allow those who had been excluded once a second chance, in the hope that they would have matured enough for a second opportunity to be worthwhile. In fact, of the five who were given a second chance, only one, a young woman, completed the programme; but there were still some signs of positive personal development in this group of excluded young people. Although only three were not convicted or charged in the year after starting at CueTen, none had accumulated as long a record of offending as some of those in the group who left the programme for other reasons, and only two were known to have spent time in custody. One successfully completed Apex's programme for adults and obtained a regular job; one went on to attend college and had a period in work; a third was working regularly at the end of the evaluation period. While these results are not dramatic, they do suggest that exclusion from CueTen did not necessarily predict a disastrous outcome; it is possible that some of these young people, who had been unable to adjust their behaviour to meet the demands of CueTen, were later able to reflect constructively on the experience, and manage the transition to employment and its disciplines, presumably, in the process, loosening their ties to subcultures of delinquency and drug use.

Levels of subsequent offending were certainly lower among the 29 young people who completed (or nearly completed) the CueTen programme in the first seven groups, and their levels of participation in further education and employment seem to have been higher than for those who did not complete the programme. Twelve certainly went on to further education or training (a relevant measure of success for Apex), and eleven, including four of those who went on to further training, spent some time in paid work, although only five seem to have settled into a stable work pattern. Seven of this group were supposed to return to school, but only one ever did so, and this was after a period in residential care. Continuing disruption in their family relationships was a factor that made life after CueTen problematic for many of these young people. We identified two young people who were given direct help by relatives in getting employment, and no doubt there were other instances of help from family members, but there is also no doubt that most members of this group of completers, as in the groups who left early or were excluded, had to cope with serious stress in their domestic lives during their time at CueTen – and the project staff were rarely able to give direct help with the resulting problems.

At Freagarrach, we obtained information on outcomes other than offending on 94 young people, but nine of these, one a young woman, had never really engaged with the project staff, so only scanty information was available about their lives after they had been accepted at Freagarrach, apart from their records of criminal charges and convictions. Four of these young people were to have attended Freagarrach as part of the process of reintegration after periods in residential care, and several had serious problems associated with heroin use: these circumstances may explain their failure to accept what the project had to offer. One was one of two young men accepted by the project who died of a heroin overdose during the evaluation period; a third died of leukaemia. It was noteworthy, when the criminal records were examined, that six of this group of nine had subsequently served at least one custodial sentence (one had served five such sentences, and another four). Overall, only 17 of the young people who had attended Freagarrach were known to have been sentenced to custody by the summer of 2000, so that young people who did not engage were at a significantly greater risk of a custodial sentence than the Freagarrach population as a whole. Inability or unwillingness to accept help in avoiding an adult criminal career seems, as at CueTen, to have been a good predictor of embarking on such a career.

Like the young people at CueTen, those at Freagarrach faced an inherent difficulty in finding a place in the labour market. For them, the difficulties facing all young people without obvious marketable skills or educational achievements were compounded by their criminal records, in some cases serious and lengthy enough to alarm any potential employer. Participation in the labour market is sometimes regarded as the key measure of social inclusion, not only for known offenders but for other marginalised groups (Smith and Stewart, 1998), but some of the young people who left Freagarrach seem to have found satisfaction in ways of life that did not entail either paid work or persistent offending (at least of a serious kind). As mentioned in Chapter 4, there were hints in the course of the evaluation that some young people – especially young men – had access to a variety of subcultural adaptations to a social and economic environment in which traditional patterns of male working class life were no longer available. Sociological commentators have discussed such adaptations in the light of the disappearance of traditional, male working class employment, sometimes positively, stressing the possibility of new, more equal social and family relationships (Giddens, 1994), but more often negatively, stressing the emergence of subcultures of aggressive masculinity, often associated with heavy drug and alcohol use, in areas where the impact of economic change has been most sharply felt (Robins, 1992; Campbell, 1993). Some of the young people who left Freagarrach seem to have experienced these new possibilities as sufficiently enticing to make a conscious decision not to work, preferring an apparently relaxed way of life that involved much contact with peers and heavy cannabis use, but no or little known criminal activity. Such a way of life, passive and drifting rather than active or aggressive, was a possibility – at least in the medium-term – in those parts of central Scotland in which traditional values, including a work ethic, were no longer a strong influence. As a way of life, it is unlikely to earn the approval of conventional society, but it is a mellower and less dangerous expression of masculinity than those described by Campbell and Robins.

In other parts of the region, particularly council housing estates in which the male labour force had formerly been largely employed in a single industry, such as mining, a more traditional set of values had survived, and provided an accessible cultural resource for some of the young people who left Freagarrach. The dominant ethic in these areas, for men, was one that placed a high valuation on both work and the heavy consumption, especially at weekends, of alcohol. Young men for whom this resource was an option were essentially embracing the same cultural values as their fathers' generation. Only fifteen (18 per cent), including one young woman, of the 83 young people who had spent a substantial period at Freagarrach by the end of 1999 and were of an age to be employed were known to be in employment at that time, or to have spent a substantial period in work before then. This figure probably understates the actual level of involvement in work of these young people, since information was not available on all cases; but when a young person was known to have substantial work experience, this was associated with a lower rate of offending, and less serious offences, since starting at Freagarrach than for the group as a whole: only one of this group had been sentenced to custody by the spring of 2000. The young people often obtained employment through family connections rather than through the formal systems designed to help those seeking work.

Apart from those who had chosen not to work, there was also a small group of young people who attended Freagarrach who were described by the staff as effectively unemployable. Given that the staff did not make such adverse judgements lightly, the claim deserves to be taken literally. Five young people were recorded as having learning difficulties serious enough to make employment problematic: the difficulties were reflected not only in cognitive limitations but in serious deficits in attention, to the point in one case of being unable to sit still; the other young people also showed a lack of basic social skills, in varying degrees. There was, however, no evidence that members of this group were particularly likely to go on to serious criminal careers; supportive parenting appeared to be an important protective factor.

At the end of 1999 three young people were known to be on training courses, and others had of course gone through various training experiences, including that provided by the Apex FVYPER project. The difficulties many of the young people had in sustaining motivation for training were discussed in Chapter 3, but it is also worth stressing that a minority of them were able to use training opportunities well enough to achieve useful qualifications and enhance their chances in the labour market. In different ways, two young people showed their capacity to make positive social contributions, one as a volunteer helper of a disabled university student in Wales, the other as a promising speedway rider. Offending after starting at Freagarrach was minimal in both cases.

Freagarrach's access to educational resources was a crucial element in the original planning of the project as part of an overall strategy for young offenders, but over the five years of the evaluation this became less important, as the average age of the young people at the project increased, and school-based education was therefore relevant for a smaller proportion. It is also likely that the aim of reintegration into mainstream schools came to seem less feasible or even desirable as an aim of work even for young people still legally subject to compulsory education; in this respect Freagarrach's experience was similar to CueTen's. It was rare for young people to be attending school normally when they started at Freagarrach, and rare for a move into normal schooling to be achieved during their time at the project. More typically, combined educational 'packages' were worked out with schools, special units, and home tutoring staff. Well over half of the young people of school age were excluded from school when they started at the project, and about another quarter were truanting; and during their time at the project, some educational provision was organised for the great majority of the relevant group of young people. Freagarrach had some success, then, in conjunction with education staff, in making arrangements that might improve the young people's educational chances, even though full-time attendance at a mainstream school was rarely achieved (or attempted); perhaps 5 per cent of the young people who were of school age attended school reasonably normally after starting at Freagarrach.

The quality of family relationships was important in the lives of the young people at Freagarrach, both in their families of origin and in the families some of them started in the period of the evaluation. Promising results in terms both of offending and of other indicators of social adjustment were associated with supportive parenting in at least seven cases, and no doubt there were more. Equally, negative relationships with parents – to the point of overt rejection, violence or abuse – were often associated with less positive outcomes. In 24 cases attendance at Freagarrach was noted as having made a difference to the young person's experience of local authority care, by removing the need for it altogether in some cases, and in others by shortening the period that would otherwise have been spent in care, delaying entry into the care system, or enabling the substitution of foster care for residential care, or of children's home accommodation for a secure unit. In another ten cases, attendance at the project was recorded as having had an effect on the need for residential schooling, removing it altogether in some cases, curtailing it in others. Freagarrach therefore contributed to the reintegration of young people into their families and local communities, although, as noted above, some of the young people who were most difficult to engage in the project's work were in some form of residential care at the time of their referral. Freagarrach's impact on the use of care and residential education is discussed further in Chapter 7, dealing with costs and benefits.

Five of the nine young women on whom information was collected at the end of 1999 were known to have had a baby by this time; in at least two of these cases it appeared that this event had improved the young women's relationships with their mothers, support perhaps being more acceptable in a grandparental than in a parental capacity. These young women had typically been sophisticated shoplifters when they came to Freagarrach, and would have been at risk of custody had they persisted with this rate of offending. In fact only one was recorded as having received a custodial sentence, for breach of probation; all but one had continued to offend, but at a substantially reduced rate. Of the other four young women, one (who did not engage with the project) had received a custodial sentence as a result of an increased rate of offending after her formal acceptance at the project; another went into residential care (with her sisters) as a result of abuse within the family during her time at Freagarrach, and was convicted of further offences on her return home; another had been in care (again as a result of abuse) when she came to Freagarrach, and had a record of frequent violence against care staff. The project staff helped her to deal with her anger about her experiences in care, and she found a job, but suffered from mental health problems, which were regarded as a more serious issue than her offending. The fourth of these young women would probably have been sent into residential care had it not been for Freagarrach; she had no recorded offences after starting at the project, despite coming from a family believed to be heavily involved in crime.

Six of the young men who attended Freagarrach were known to have become fathers by the end of 1999, and another had been a father, at the age of fourteen, before he started at Freagarrach. According to social control theory and research on criminal careers, the birth of a child should encourage desistance from serious or persistent offending (Hirschi, 1969; Leibrich, 1993; Sampson and Laub, 1993). There was some suggestion that becoming a mother had had this effect on the offending of the young women discussed above, and three of the young men who had become fathers had very few or no convictions or charges recorded against them after leaving

Freagarrach, while the offending rate of another showed a marked decline after the age of seventeen. The remaining two who were known to have become fathers, however, had among the worst records of offending after their time at Freagarrach of the entire group, essentially continuing after their attendance in much the same vein as before it; so it is clear that the birth of a child does not invariably increase commitment to conventional lines of behaviour. It is possible that a milestone such as the birth of a child has less of a protective effect than suggested by previous research in a context of high local unemployment, low wages for those who do manage to obtain jobs, and poor economic prospects (Stewart et al., 1994; Graham and Bowling, 1995); but this is not to say that the protective effect disappears completely.

In summary, the information available on the life-courses of the young people who left Freagarrach (apart from their offending careers) is limited in most cases, but what is known suggests that an initial failure to engage with the project, through apathy or active rejection, was associated with a poor outcome in terms of reconvictions. Young people who did engage with the project over a period of at least three months were presumably better motivated to make changes in their lives and to see Freagarrach as a possible source of worthwhile help; willingness to consider change is a necessary precursor to actually changing. Information on employment was incomplete, but there were indications that substantial experience of paid work was associated with a lower rate of, and less serious, offending than for the group as a whole. The younger members of the Freagarrach group, for whom the immediate goal was a return to some form of education rather than a move into work, generally showed positive changes during their time at Freagarrach, although it was rare for them to move into full-time mainstream education. Support from parents or other relatives was important as a predictor of positive adjustment to the demands of adult life, and young people who had children by the end of 1999 generally – but not invariably – showed lower rates of offending than the group as a whole. In all these associations cause and effect are hard to untangle: for example, the ability to get and keep a job may reflect the same variable – motivation to change or commitment to conventional activity – as a reduced rate of offending, and parental or other family support may be a response to improvements in the young person's behaviour as well as (or instead of) causing them. Nevertheless, the information available on outcomes other than offending suggests that a constellation of factors, including employment, training and a supportive family, is associated with a reduced risk of offending – a point that has implications for policy and practice designed to reinforce positive elements of the social and economic environment of juvenile offenders.

Sources and Interpretation of Reoffending Data

Here we discuss some problems in interpreting our figures on reoffending, and in particular the difficulty of making valid comparisons between the criminal careers of the young people at the projects and young offenders who received other forms of intervention. While some suggestive comparisons did emerge, these should be treated as just that – suggestive rather than definitive – and conclusions from them should be regarded as tentative.

For the young people at CueTen, information on offending before starting at the project came from the records of the Fife police, who also provided access to Scottish Criminal Records Office (SCRO) records for the follow-up data. Two-year follow-up data were obtained for the first three CueTen intakes (the third group having started in September 1996), and one-year data for the next three (the sixth group having started in September 1997). The police also provided details on young offenders in Fife with comparable records of being charged as juveniles, but who did not attend CueTen. Information on this group was also obtained from the Area Reporter. Four young people originally in this group later attended CueTen, and additional cases were then sought from the police, to maintain a comparison group of a reasonable size; seven young people from these additional cases eventually attended CueTen, producing a final comparison group of 39 young people, five of them young women. This group included some young people who were in fact accepted by CueTen but for some reason did not attend, even for a day; the reasons were usually that they were placed in residential care, or that they absconded from an existing care placement. The comparison group was closely matched on age and gender with the CueTen group, the proportions of males and females, and of 14 and 15 year olds, being virtually identical; and they had similar characteristics to the CueTen group in respect of their offending and referrals to the Reporter on other grounds. Two-year data were available for 18 members of the comparison group, and one-year data for the remaining 21.

The young people in the comparison group who failed to start at CueTen because of absconding or a residential requirement might be considered worse risks than at least some of the CueTen population, and therefore to bias the comparison group towards worse predicted outcomes; on the other hand, since CueTen did in general work with the most persistent young offenders in Fife, the proportion of young people in the comparison group in the least persistent category (with five or fewer charges in a 12-month period) was higher than in the CueTen group (20 of the 39 (51 per cent) being in this category, as opposed to 22 (37 per cent) of the 59 young people who attended CueTen in the first six intakes). Twenty-five (43 per cent) of the CueTen group were in the middle category (six to 15 charges), compared with twelve (31 per cent) of the comparison group; and the figures for the most persistent category are twelve (20 per cent) for the CueTen group and seven (18 per cent) for the comparison group. The biases in the comparison group may almost be considered as cancelling each other out: it contained a higher proportion of low risk, but also some very high risk, young people. The differences between the two groups in terms of the proportions in the 'five or fewer charges' and the 'six charges and over' categories are not statistically significant, but it should be borne in mind that if anything the comparison group may overall consist of young people at a slightly lower risk of reoffending than the CueTen group.

In interpreting the data presented below on reoffending, it is important to remember that reconviction data are not the same as reoffending data; but they are usually regarded as an acceptable proxy measure for reoffending, and some of the problems in using and interpreting reconviction rates discussed by Mair et al. (1997) do not apply to the CueTen sample: because of the age of the group, there should be very few if any false positives (convictions arising from offences committed before the young person started the programme). Where information is given on offending in the year before starting at CueTen or before inclusion in the comparison group, this takes the form of charges referred to the Reporter; subsequent offending is usually measured by convictions as recorded by the SCRO, but for some of the younger offenders charges referred to the Reporter are also included, as additional information or as the best available measure of offending. Where possible, for both CueTen and Freagarrach groups, we try to show the extent and nature of reoffending rather than simply noting whether or not the young people reoffended. As will become clear, when a period of at least two years after starting at the projects is considered, it was rare for young people not to be known to have reoffended at all.

For Freagarrach, material on reoffending came from two main sources: Scottish Criminal Records and the TRACE system. The former (in the form made available for the research) gave data on convictions, pending charges, and Children's Hearing System decisions (all decisions were recorded for juveniles, only those that changed the young person's legal status for those aged 16 and over); TRACE gave all charges made against juveniles in the central Scotland police area, up to a maximum of five charges for each incident that gave rise to a charge. The criminal records provided data that allow for comparisons both with other studies and with two comparison groups, the CueTen comparison group and one obtained specifically for the Freagarrach evaluation. Neither group was composed overall of as serious and persistent offenders as the Freagarrach population, which limits the usefulness of comparisons, and a further limitation is that information from TRACE was not comparable either with other studies or with the comparison group data, since the system was unique to Central Scotland Police; it is useful, however, in giving an indication of changes in the volume and nature of suspected offending by young people after they started at Freagarrach – 'suspected', because the young people were not necessarily guilty of all the offences with which they were charged, and some charges would never have progressed further in the criminal justice process, because of evidential and other considerations. Since a project should be judged by its failures as well as its successes, no distinction is drawn in the analysis of reoffending after attendance at Freagarrach between young people who spent a substantial period at the project and those who never engaged with it; and, in view of the open-ended and flexible nature of the Freagarrach programme, we have not distinguished between 'completers' and 'non-completers', as was possible in the CueTen evaluation.

The comparison group found specifically for Freagarrach was only identified after prolonged negotiations with the police and other agencies in various parts of Scotland, and came from data held by the Reporter's Administration on juveniles in another part of the central belt of Scotland.[1] This produced a total of 52 young people who at some time in their lives had accumulated five or more charges in a 12-month period, and were roughly matched in terms of age and gender with the Freagarrach group; their criminal records were analysed for the period January 1998–December 2000. In addition, the comparison group of 39 young people used for the evaluation of CueTen was used in assessing the relative performance of Freagarrach, in order

---

1   A comparison group could not be found in central Scotland, since the great majority of persistent juvenile offenders there attended Freagarrach.

to produce a total comparison group similar in size to the Freagarrach group. Sixty-three (66 per cent) of the young people at Freagarrach had been charged by the age of twelve; the comparable figure for the central belt comparison group was 20 out of 52, or 38 per cent. Twenty-nine (30 per cent) of the Freagarrach young people were in the lowest risk group, with five or fewer charges or convictions in the year before they started at the project, compared with 36 (69 per cent) of the comparison group (and 51 per cent of the group used for the CueTen evaluation). On average, young people attending Freagarrach had ten charges or convictions against them in the previous 12 months (using Scottish Criminal Records data), while the central belt comparison group averaged four. These and other differences mean that a direct comparison is liable to be misleadingly to Freagarrach's disadvantage, since the Freagarrach young people – as a whole – were a higher risk group for subsequent offending than either of the other groups; they were also a higher risk group – again as a whole – than the young people who attended the CueTen project.

Slightly anticipating the discussion of Freagarrach's effectiveness, we can note here that of the young people in the Freagarrach group on whom two-year follow-up data were available a lower proportion had five or fewer charges or convictions in this period, and a higher proportion over 20, than in the comparison groups; but the differences were not statistically significant, and in fact a slightly higher proportion of the combined comparison groups had over 30 charges or convictions during the two years. Statistically non-significant differences – not all to Freagarrach's disadvantage – were also found between the Freagarrach group and the comparison groups (and the CueTen group itself) in comparing the total numbers of offences (from Scottish Criminal Records) before and after the date at which the young people began attending the projects or were included in a comparison group. Given the higher rate of prior offending in the Freagarrach group, it is perhaps surprising that no statistically significant differences were found – a result that could be interpreted as evidence that Freagarrach made more of a positive difference relative to the range of measures to which the other groups were subject.

Some interesting comparative information emerges when the criminal careers of the Freagarrach young people are measured against those from the comparison groups, using severity of sentence as a proxy for offence seriousness. A higher proportion of the young people who were convicted or charged in the combined comparison group (the central belt group and the CueTen comparison group) were sentenced to custody during the two-year period for which records are available. Of the 67 young people with convictions or charges in this group, nineteen (28 per cent) were sentenced to custody, compared with twelve (14 per cent) of the 83 young people (over a two-year period) charged or convicted in the Freagarrach group. The 19 young people in the comparison group received a total of 28 custodial sentences; two sentences were for murder, one was for five years, one for three years, two for two years, and one for 18 months. The 12 young people in the Freagarrach group received 25 custodial sentences in the comparable two-year period, the longest of which was for six years; one was for 18 months and one for a year, and fifteen of the 25 sentences were for three months or less. A smaller proportion of the Freagarrach young people, then, received custodial sentences in the two years after they started at the project, compared with the comparison group, and those who were sentenced to custody tended to receive shorter terms. There are indications, therefore, that Freagarrach may have produced a lower risk of custody than would otherwise have been the case; if the same proportion of the Freagarrach group had been sentenced to custody as in the comparison group, 23 rather than 12 would have received such sentences over the two-year period. The difference between the groups is statistically significant at the 5 per cent level, but it cannot be claimed confidently that all of the difference is due to Freagarrach, since the sentences were imposed at different times and in different courts. It is likely, however, that Freagarrach contributed a proportion of the difference, since there were no major variations in sentencing practice across the relevant courts in 1997, the latest year in the relevant period for which figures were available (Scottish Office, 1999).

Reoffending After Starting at CueTen

Table 6.1 gives aggregate figures for reconvictions in the 12-month period after starting at CueTen or inclusion in the comparison group, separating those who completed the programme and those who did not. This and the following tables on CueTen exclude one young man who died before completing the programme.

Table 6.1 CueTen: reconvictions after 12 months (completers, non-completers and comparison group)

	Number of reconvictions				
Group	*None*	*1–5*	*6–15*	*16 or more*	*Total*
Completers	10 (42%)	10 (42%)	3 (12%)	1 (4%)	24
Non-completers	11 (32%)	4 (12%)	12 (35%)	7 (21%)	34
Comparison group	10 (26%)	16 (41%)	9 (23%)	4 (10%)	39

Overall, the differences between the groups shown in Table 6.1, while interesting, do not reach statistical significance. Bearing in mind that the young people who completed the programme were, as a group, less persistent offenders than those who did not complete, and that only one of them had been charged more than 16 times in the previous 12 months, compared with seven of the comparison group, it would be unwise to claim from these figures that CueTen had demonstrated an effect in the desired direction; rather, the groups' subsequent reconviction rates broadly reflected their previous offending rates, with the most persistent offender group being most likely to accumulate the most subsequent convictions. Table 6.2 presents the comparable figures at the 24-month point, for the smaller number of cases for which these are available.

Table 6.2 CueTen: reconvictions after 24 months (completers, non-completers and comparison group)

	Number of reconvictions				
Group	None	1–5	6–15	16 or more	Total
Completers	3 (20%)	7 (47%)	1 (7%)	4 (26%)	15
Non-completers	1 (7%)	3 (21%)	5 (36%)	5 (36%)	14
Comparison group	1 (6%)	4 (22%)	8 (44%)	5 (28%)	18

The same general pattern appears as in Table 6.1, with a higher proportion – two-thirds – of the completers group than of the others appearing in the first two columns. Again, though, the differences are not statistically significant, and the proportions of each group who after 24 months had been convicted for over 15 offences are similar; in respect of the group of completers, one might interpret their apparent 'catching up' with the other groups as suggesting the erosion of a treatment effect from CueTen, but with such small numbers this can only be a speculation. Taken together, these two tables suggest that persistent juvenile offenders are most unlikely not to be convicted as young adults: only five of the 47 young people in Table 6.2 had not been convicted at all in the two years under review. It is, however, quite possible for 12 months to pass without a conviction being recorded – 31 of the 97 young people in Table 6.1 had no recorded convictions; and presumably this is partly because of the lapses of time between offending and conviction, and between a conviction and its appearance in the SCRO record, and partly because most of these young people only became eligible to be convicted during the first 12 months, when they reached the age of sixteen. The figures do not require the assumption of any treatment effect or of its erosion over time, and provide a reminder of the limitations of reconviction rates, especially over a short time period and with a juvenile population, as a measure of offending.

These aggregate data convey nothing of the course of individual criminal careers; nor do they say anything about the seriousness of the offences for which these young people were convicted. The following three detailed tables present in summary form the criminal careers over both 12 months and, where possible, two years, of those who completed the CueTen programme, those who did not, and the comparison group. Each table gives, for each young person, the number of charges referred to the Reporter in the previous 12 months, and the number of subsequent charges and convictions, and indicates, where this was known, the most severe penalty imposed to date (a commonly used proxy measure for offence seriousness). Where a subsequent offence was particularly serious, this is noted. In the case of four of the completers who reoffended, and who had a substantial record of earlier offending, there had been no known offending for at least a year, so there were some grounds for optimism about the likely development of an adult criminal career. (The time lapse problem noted above is much less of an issue with charges than with convictions.)

These tables are illuminating in several ways. Firstly, they show that there is nothing inevitable about the development of an adult criminal career, even after persistent offending as a juvenile, and that sometimes criminal careers develop after a modest history of juvenile offending. While there is an obvious positive relationship between the number of charges before the follow-up period and the number of charges and convictions during it, all three tables show striking exceptions to this rule. For instance, Table 6.3 shows that one of the CueTen completers, who had been charged only once in the previous 12 months, was convicted 26 times in the second year of the follow-up period, and that two of the most persistent juvenile offenders in this group, each with 15 charges in the 12 months before starting at CueTen, were each known to have offended only once in the subsequent 24 months. Equally or more striking are the case in Table 6.4 of the young person with 41 charges in the 12 months before starting who was not known to have offended at all in the following two years, and the case in Table 6.5 of the young person with six charges in the 12 months before starting who accumulated 26 charges referred to the Reporter and six convictions in the following year. Table 6.5 also provides a dramatic example of the limitations of using the number of convictions alone[2] as a measure of criminality, since the two cases in which a young person was convicted of murder would appear, on the offence count measure, as successes; in one case the murder conviction was the only one in the 12 month follow-up period, after 25 charges in the previous year. All the tables also provide examples of young people whose subsequent offending was minimal in the first 12 months of the follow-up period and substantial in the second 12 months, and *vice versa*.

---

2   Or number of court appearances at which there was a finding of guilt.

Table 6.3 CueTen completers: charges, convictions and sentences

Charges in previous 12 months	Number of young people (Total 24)	Charges and convictions since starting at CueTen over 12 and 24 months
None	2	(a) 1 charge to the Reporter (12 months) (b) 2 charges to the Reporter (12 months); 3 convictions: probation (24 months)
1	2	(a) 1 charge to the Reporter (12 months) (b) 3 charges to the Reporter (12 months); 26 convictions: custody (24 months)
2	2	(a) 10 charges to the Reporter; 2 convictions (12 months) (b) no convictions (12 months)
3	3	(a) 2 charges to the Reporter (12 months); 3 convictions (24 months) (b) no convictions (12 months); 1 conviction (24 months) (c) 2 charges to the Reporter (12 months); no convictions (24 months)
4	3	(a) no convictions (24 months) (b) no convictions (24 months) (c) 4 charges to the Reporter (12 months)
5	1	no convictions (24 months)
6	1	5 charges to the Reporter (12 months); 13 convictions: probation (24 months)
7	2	(a) 17 charges to the Reporter (12 months); 1 charge to the Reporter (24 months) (b) 2 charges to the Reporter (12 months); 2 charges to the Reporter (24 months)
8	2	(a) no convictions (12 months); 26 convictions: probation (24 months) (b) 7 charges to the Reporter (12 months)
10	2	(a) no convictions (12 months); 9 convictions: probation (24 months)
11	1	5 charges to the Reporter (12 months)
15	2	(a) 1 charge to the Reporter (12 months); no convictions (24 months) (b) no convictions (12 months); 1 conviction (24 months)
26	1	7 charges to the Reporter (12 months)

Total Charges

155		155 convictions/charges (70 after 12 months)

Table 6.4 CueTen non-completers: charges, convictions and sentences

Charges in previous 12 months	Number of young people (Total 35)	Charges and convictions since starting at CueTen over 12 and 24 months
None	1	no convictions (12 months)
1	1	no convictions (12 months)
2	1	6 charges to the Reporter (12 months); 2 convictions (24 months)
3	1	6 charges to the Reporter and 1 conviction (12 months); 8 convictions (24 months)
4	4	(a) 1 charge to the Reporter and 1 conviction (12 months) (b) no convictions (12 months) (c) no convictions (12 months) (d) no convictions (12 months)
5	1	21 convictions: two custodial sentences (12 months)
7	2	(a) 15 charges to the Reporter and 3 convictions (12 months) (b) 7 convictions: custodial sentence (12 months)
8	2	(a) no convictions (12 months) (b) 11 charges to the Reporter (12 months)
9	4	(a) 6 charges to the Reporter (12 months); 3 convictions (24 months) (b) 51 convictions: 2 custodial sentences (12 months) (c) 1 conviction (12 months) (d) no convictions (12 months)
11	1	8 charges to the Reporter (12 months); 17 convictions: community service order (24 months)
12	3	(a) died (b) no convictions (12 months) (c) 16 charges to the Reporter and 15 convictions: custodial sentence (12 months)
13	3	(a) 3 convictions: community service order (12 months) (b) no convictions (12 months); 2 convictions (24 months) (c) 8 convictions: probation (12 months)
17	2	(a) 12 convictions (12 months); 4 convictions: custodial sentence (24 months) (b) 7 charges to the Reporter and 3 convictions: probation (12 months)
20	1	7 charges to the Reporter and 7 convictions: probation (12 months)
21	1	15 convictions (12 months); 15 convictions: community service order (24 months)
26	2	(a) no convictions (12 months); 8 convictions: probation (24 months) (b) 9 convictions (12 months); 6 convictions: custody (5 years: robbery) (24 months)
27	1	1 conviction (12 months); 3 convictions (24 months)
36	2	(a) 18 convictions: custodial sentence (12 months); 20 convictions: probation (24 months) (b) 25 convictions: 3 custodial sentences (12 months)
41	1	no convictions (24 months)
45	1	32 convictions: custodial sentence (12 months); 30 convictions: custodial sentence (24 months)

Total Charges

491		436 convictions/charges (316 after 12 months)

Table 6.5 CueTen comparison group: charges, convictions and sentences

Charges in previous 12 months	Number of young people (Total 39)	Charges and convictions since inclusion in comparison group over 12 and 24 months
None	1	no convictions (12 months)
1	2	(a) 1 conviction (12 months) (b) no convictions (12 months); 8 convictions (24 months)
2	3	(a) 2 charges to the Reporter (12 months); no convictions (24 months) (b) 5 convictions: custodial sentence (12 months) (c) no convictions (12 months)
3	5	(a) 5 charges to the Reporter (12 months); 1 conviction (24 months) (b) no convictions (12 months) (c) 3 charges to the Reporter (12 months) (d) 8 convictions (12 months) (e) 8 convictions: custodial sentence (3 years: robbery) (12 months)
4	6	(a) 2 convictions (12 months); 7 convictions: custodial sentence (24 months) (b) 3 convictions (12 months); 1 conviction (24 months) (c) 3 charges to the Reporter (12 months) (d) 2 convictions (12 months) (e) 3 convictions (12 months) (f) no convictions (12 months)
5	3	(a) no convictions (12 months) (b) 1 conviction (12 months) (c) 2 convictions (12 months)
6	3	(a) 26 charges to the Reporter and 6 convictions (12 months); 4 convictions (24 months) (b) no convictions (12 months) (c) no convictions (24 months)
7	3	(a) 9 charges to the Reporter (12 months); 2 convictions (24 months) (b) 6 charges to the Reporter (12 months); 3 convictions (24 months) (c) 3 charges to the Reporter and 3 convictions (12 months)
8	3	(a) no convictions (12 months); 5 convictions (24 months) (b) 1 charge to the Reporter (12 months); no convictions (24 months) (c) 10 convictions (12 months)
9	1	20 charges to the Reporter (12 months); 4 charges to the Reporter (24 months)
10	1	no convictions (12 months)
11	1	10 charges to the Reporter (12 months); no convictions (24 months)
18	1	2 convictions (12 months); 13 convictions (24 months)
20	1	12 convictions (12 months); 11 convictions: custodial sentence (24 months)
22	1	3 convictions: custodial sentence (12 months); 7 convictions: probation (24 months)
23	1	21 convictions: custodial sentence (12 months); 6 convictions: custody (life: murder) (24 months)
25	1	1 conviction: custody (life: murder) (12 months)
26	1	14 charges to the Reporter (12 months); 28 convictions: 2 custodial sentences (24 months)
31	1	20 convictions (12 months)

Total Charges

320		315 convictions/charges (215 after 12 months)

The tables allow for a before and after analysis of the offending pattern of each individual, and of the groups as a whole. Table 6.3 shows that fifteen of the 24 young people who completed the programme had fewer offences recorded against them in the follow-up period than in the previous 12 months; in eight of these cases, where the young person had been subsequently charged or convicted at least once, there was still evidence that their rate of offending was decreasing over time, and only one appeared to show a pattern of escalating offending. One young person continued to offend at the same rate as before, in the sense that there were as many recorded offences in the 12 months following his start at CueTen as in the 12 months prior to it, but he had had no offences recorded against him for over a year at the time of the analysis. The offending rate of eight of the young people had increased in the follow-up period, in five cases substantially; six of these cases showed an apparent escalation of offending, one (with 17 charges in the first year but only one in the second) showed a diminishing rate, and one (a low rate offender) had hardly changed. Overall, the table suggests that 16 of these young people had a reduced rate of offending after starting at CueTen, or continued to offend at the same low level, while the offending rate of seven had escalated. Only one of these young people had received a custodial sentence, suggesting that even in the cases of persistent offending after starting at CueTen the offences were in general not especially serious.

Table 6.4, covering those who did not complete the programme, shows that, although on an offence count alone perhaps 20 of these 34 young people (excluding the one who died) could be thought of as having a slower rate of offending in the follow-up period than in the previous 12 months, when seriousness and absolute rate of offending are taken into account it would be sensible to conclude that only 13 appeared to be unlikely to go on to a serious criminal career as adults. These are the cases where there was no known subsequent offending, where it was minimal, and where there was a marked reduction in the rate of conviction (as in the case of the young person who had been charged with 27 offences before starting at CueTen). At least 11 cases in this table show a movement in the opposite direction, with a record of offending that escalated both in frequency and seriousness; in the remaining cases, even where the frequency of offending decreased it continued to be high, or there was little change. Ten of this group (all male) had served at least one custodial sentence; three of these had served two, and one had been sentenced to custody on three separate occasions (making a total of 15 custodial sentences for this group). Table 6.5, giving figures for the comparison group, suggests that perhaps 18 of these 39 young people had low or markedly reduced rates of offending over the follow-up period, while (conservatively) 14 continued at a high rate or escalating rate; eight, all male, had received custodial sentences, two of whom had been sentenced to custody twice.

Thus far, the comparisons favour the group of young people who completed the CueTen programme, a higher proportion of whom showed signs of deceleration of or desistance from offending than in the other two groups, with the outcomes for the group who attended the CueTen programme, but did not complete it, being worse overall than for the comparison group. The three tables also give aggregated figures for the numbers of convictions and charges against each group in the year preceding the target date and for the subsequent one-year and two-year periods. It should be remembered that this is not a like-for-like comparison, since only charges are counted in the period before the target date, not all of which would have led to convictions in the adult system, while both charges (for those still in the Children's Hearings System) and convictions (for those in the adult system) are counted in the subsequent periods. In view of this, although all three groups had fewer offences recorded against them in the subsequent year than in the previous year, and, with the exception of the CueTen completers, had fewer such offences in the second year after the target date than in the first, it would not be sensible to infer from these figures either a treatment effect or a maturation effect: the proportion of recorded offences that consists of charges referred to the Reporter is much lower for the second year, since nearly all the young people had by that stage moved out of the Children's Hearings System. The basis of comparison is the same for all three groups, however, and this allows the results to be compared across the three groups. The total number of convictions and charges for the group who completed the CueTen programme in the year following their starting dates was 70, 45 per cent of the previous year's total; for the group who started at CueTen but did not finish the figure was 316, 64 per cent of the previous year's figure; and for the comparison group the figures were 215 and 67 per cent.

Table 6.6 CueTen: charges and convictions over time

Charges and convictions	12 months prior	12 months after CueTen	Second 12–month period
Completers	(N = 24)	(N = 24)	(N = 15)
Total	155	70	85
Average	6	3	6
Median	4.5	1.5	1
Non-completers	(N = 34)	(N = 34)	(N = 14)
Total	491	316	120
Average	14	9	9
Median	11	6.5	5
Comparison group	(N = 39)	(N = 39)	(N = 18)
Total	320	215	100
Average	8	5.5	6
Median	5	4	4

Over the first year, then, the CueTen completers committed less than half as many known offences as in the previous year, while the other two groups' recorded offending in the same period was at roughly two-thirds of the previous year's level. The picture changes, however, for the second year, by the end of which the CueTen completers had accumulated as many known offences as in the year before they started at the project; the two-year figure for the comparison group was virtually identical to the figure for the year preceding the target date, and the figure for the other CueTen group was slightly lower. That is, 55 per cent of the subsequent known offending of the CueTen completers' group took place (or at least was formally recorded) in the second year, compared with 28 per cent of the non-completers' offending and 32 per cent of the offending of the comparison group. Again, it is tempting to interpret this result as indicating the erosion of a treatment effect, but it should be remembered that the numbers for whom two-year follow-up data are available are small, and 52 of the 85 offences recorded against this group in the second year were the responsibility of just two young people. Table 6.6 shows the before and after pattern of offending in more detail.

The analysis above has shown that there were differences in the offending pattern of the young people who completed the CueTen programme and the other two groups. There is little doubt that the project helped some young people to modify their behaviour, and it does not require any special pleading to conclude from the figures that CueTen contributed to a reduction in both the frequency and the seriousness of offending in the group who finished the programme. Only five (just over a fifth) of this group had ten or more offences recorded against them in the follow-up period, compared with twelve (35 per cent) in the group who did not complete the programme and eleven (28 per cent) in the comparison group; and all six of the young people who had ten or more charges against them in the previous 12 months showed a reduced frequency of offending after starting at CueTen. The differences are not statistically significant, however, and it would not be sensible to claim confidently that the data on reconviction and subsequent charging demonstrate that CueTen had a lasting effect on the offending of these young people. If, however, the group who completed the programme had behaved in the same way as the other two groups, which in this respect are very similar, in the 12 months after they started at CueTen, then the figure for known offences would have been about 100, rather than 70. The two-year figures are less encouraging, but it should be remembered that two young people committed the majority of the offences recorded against members of this group in the second year, and if they are excluded then the average figure for offending in this period becomes about 2.5, lower than for the other two groups. The numbers are small, however, and it would be difficult to justify excluding these two cases, since a similar manoeuvre would also lower the average figure for the other groups. The evidence on offence seriousness is perhaps clearer: only one member of the group who completed the programme received a custodial sentence, whereas ten such sentences were imposed on members of the comparison group, and 15 on members of the group who did not finish the CueTen programme.

As noted earlier, projects ought to be judged on their apparent failures as well as their apparent successes, and the results become a good deal less encouraging when the whole group of young people who attended the project is considered against the comparison group. In fact, the group of non-completers showed the greatest relative reduction in frequency of known offending of all the groups when the final period of 12 months is compared with the first follow-up year or the year preceding the target date, but this figure will have been distorted by time spent in custody: members of this group were more likely than the comparison group to have been sentenced to a Young Offenders Institution, and fifteen of the 34 had been convicted or charged more than ten times during the follow-up period, in most cases persisting in the pattern of frequent offending they had displayed before starting at CueTen.

Speculating about possible longer-term outcomes, one can interpret Tables 6.3–6.5 as indicating that exactly half of the total CueTen population of 58 young people were offending over the follow-up period at a rate that suggests that they might well not go on to an active criminal career as adults; the same is true of just under half, eighteen out of 39, of the comparison group. In most of these cases the difference in the offending rate before and after the target date is not great enough to suggest a 'treatment' effect, but in 12 of the CueTen group, and five of the comparison group, the decrease in the level of offending is marked enough to suggest that something happened in the follow-up period to reduce the likelihood of an adult criminal career. Again, the numbers are too small and the difference between the groups not impressive enough to allow for a confident conclusion, but it is the case that a higher proportion of the CueTen group than of the comparison group showed this pattern – a substantial reduction in their rate of offending, and if this is taken to be an effect of the CueTen programme (a combination of encouraging desistance and inhibiting escalation), then CueTen might have helped to divert around one in 20 young people from an adult criminal career – or three of the 58 young people who are the subject of this discussion. This is, of course, no more than an informed guess; but such guesses are relevant if the analysis of costs, savings and benefits which follows in Chapter 7 is to attend to longer term as well as immediate issues.

Reoffending After Starting at Freagarrach

Table 6.7 shows the total number of charges and/or convictions recorded against the 95 young people for whom at least six months' follow-up data were available from the date of their formally starting to attend Freagarrach. The rows show the number of charges in eight bands; the columns the number of young people grouped by the length of the period for which information is available.

The table suggests that Freagarrach contributed to a reduction in the rate of known offending of a substantial proportion of the young people with whom it worked, but that this may have been a relatively brief 'containment' effect rather than a long-term change. Only four of the 14 young people in the six-month group showed a rate of offending similar to or higher than the rate at which they were offending when they came to Freagarrach, and the same is true of only six of the 17 young people in the 12-month group. Taking these groups together, 21 out of the 31 young people, or 68 per cent, had no charges or convictions, or between one and five, representing a considerably reduced rate of known offending in all cases. (With the six-month group, it is likely that delays in entering charges or convictions meant that some known offending had yet to be recorded; on the other hand, convictions – but not charges – during that period are likely to relate to offences committed before the young people started at Freagarrach, and therefore to be false positives or 'pseudo-reconvictions' (Mair et al., 1997) or pseudo-charges, from the point of view of the evaluation. It is probable that the two limitations in the data – both products of delay – in effect cancel each other out.)

Table 6.7 Freagarrach: number of young people subject to charges or convictions by length of follow-up period

	Length of period					
Number of charges/ convictions	6 months	12 months	2 years	3 years	4 years	Total of young people
None	6	3	3	0	0	12
1-5	4	8	4	4	1	21
6-10	3	3	6	6	1	19
11-20	0	1	4	7	7	19
21-30	0	1	5	1	5	12
31-40	1	0	1	0	3	5
41-50	0	1	0	0	2	3
51-60	0	0	0	0	4	4
Total	14	17	23	18	23	95

Taking the three groups with the longest follow-up periods, on the other hand, produces a rather different picture: in these groups, it was unusual for the young people to have no or few convictions or charges recorded against them. It is of course to be expected that the proportion convicted – and convicted of large numbers of offences – will be higher in groups with a longer follow-up period, and this pattern is clear from the table: the proportion of young people with no or few convictions or charges declines sharply, from seven out of 23 in the 2-year group, to four out of 18 in the three-year group, and one out of 23 in the group for which four years' reconviction figures are available. Equally, the proportion with many convictions or charges increases, particularly between the three-year and four-year groups: nine of the 23 young people in the latter group had been convicted or charged for over 30 offences, suggesting (though not conclusively) that they were likely to develop serious criminal careers (careers lasting 10–12 years, in Farrington's (1992) definition). The use of four-year data is unusual in evaluation research (making comparisons difficult, and disadvantaging Freagarrach relative to other projects), and the number involved is too small for confident conclusions to be drawn, but a possible interpretation of these figures is that even when young people were influenced in the desired direction by attendance at Freagarrach, the power of that influence waned over time in most cases, perhaps as a result of the lack of supportive networks in their lives that might have reinforced and maintained the benefits gained from the project (Raynor and Vanstone, 1996).

This interpretation of the data is at first sight at odds with the results of an analysis of the time interval to the first charge or conviction after young people started at Freagarrach. Of the 83 young people with some offence recorded against them, 75 were charged or convicted within the first six months, four in the next six months, and four in the following year. The six-month figures will, however, have been skewed by pseudo-reconvictions, and the relevant question is not whether attendance at Freagarrach led to complete desistance from offending (although it seems to have helped in this in some cases, over the medium-term), but whether it helped to produce a reduced rate of offending. The 81 young people on whom at least 12 months' figures are available had a total of 801 charges or convictions against them in the year before starting at Freagarrach, and 681 in the year after starting, a reduction of 15 per cent in the total volume of recorded offending; the true percentage reduction will have been somewhat higher, since some of the early convictions will relate to earlier offences. Mair et al. (1997) suggest a discount of around 6 per cent to allow for false positives in assessing the effectiveness of community penalties, but since the figures for the Freagarrach population include charges as well as convictions this discount is likely to be too high. It is still possible to conclude, from these figures, that the overall offending rate in this group could be as much as 20 per cent lower in the year after starting at Freagarrach than in the year before.

Another measure of the impact of Freagarrach on the young people's subsequent offending is to count not the total number of convictions or charges, as in Table 6.7, but the number of court appearances at which they were convicted of an offence, and the number of Children's Hearings at which an offence ground for the referral was accepted. Using this measure, as in Table 6.8, produces a picture that helps to put into perspective the rather negative long-term outcomes shown in Table 6.7. While the pattern is the same as in the earlier table, Table 6.8 suggests that a very high frequency of court appearances was unusual, even for the group on whom four years' records are available. It should be remembered that Table 6.7 included charges and convictions for all offences, and that some were relatively trivial, and others entailed by the nature of the main offence (for example, unauthorised taking of motor vehicles entails driving without insurance). Other charges might well never have led to prosecution or conviction.

Twelve of the 23 young people with records for four years had been sentenced (or received a disposal from a Children's Hearing) on fewer than six occasions, as had 13 of the 18 young people in the three-year group; on the other hand, three of the 4-year group had received a sentence or other disposal on more than ten occasions. Whether the figures in the table are counted as evidence of success or failure depends on one's sense of the context: these were, generally speaking, the most prolific juvenile offenders in central Scotland at the time of their arrival at Freagarrach, and therefore the young people for whom a long criminal career could most reasonably be predicted. The fact that only three of the 41 with a follow-up period of at least three years had been sentenced on more than ten occasions could be taken as encouraging evidence that the most pessimistic projections of their future careers at the time of their arrival at Freagarrach were not realised.

Table 6.8 Freagarrach: number of young people involved in court appearances and hearings by length of follow-up period

	Number of young people, by length of follow-up					
Number of court appearances/ hearings	*6 months*	*12 months*	*2 years*	*3 years*	*4 years*	*Total of young people*
None	11	5	4	1	1	22
1–2	2	6	6	6	4	24
3–5	0	5	10	6	7	28
6–10	1	1	2	5	8	17
11–20	0	0	1	0	2	3
21+	0	0	0	0	1	1
Total	14	17	23	18	23	95

The rate of offending provides only one indication of the criminality of these young people; another crucial measure concerns the type of offences they committed. The analysis of their careers based on court appearances could be distorted if, for example, many of the young people had committed a few very serious offences, leading to long periods in custody: in fact, one young man was convicted of murder at his only court appearance. Offence seriousness is to an extent a subjective matter, which is why the nature of the sentences imposed is often taken as a reliable proxy measure of seriousness. Table 6.9 shows the most severe sentence or order imposed on the 83 young people who had been convicted of some offence, or admitted an offence ground of referral.

In all, 38 custodial sentences were imposed on these young people; one custodial sentence was a good predictor of another. Seven of the 17 young people sent to custody,[3] including two young women, served only one sentence; two served five such sentences, another two served four, one served three, and five served two. The longest sentence was of life, for murder; the next longest were two six-year sentences, for serious assaults, in one case sexual. Three other sentences were for 12 months or more, all for offences of violence. The remaining sentences ranged in length from seven days (for breach of the peace) to ten months (for attempting to pervert the course of justice). Most sentences were short: a three-month sentence was imposed on ten occasions, and 13 sentences were of two months or less. More than half of these short sentences were for crimes of dishonesty; the rest were mainly for assault and breach of the peace. Looked at from another angle, Table 6.9 shows that 66 of these young people had not committed offences of such quantity or gravity as to lead to a custodial sentence; only seven of the four-year group of 23, and three of the three-year group of eighteen, had been sentenced to custody during a

---

3   Among whom were six of the nine young people who never engaged with what Freagarrach had to offer. One of these received five custodial sentences, and another four.

period of their lives when, as young adults, they were still in a high risk category for offending. At the other end of the scale, eight of the 61 young people with at least two years' follow-up data had received a minimal disposal as their most severe penalty (no action, a warning from the police or an admonishment from a sheriff, or the continuation of an existing order). For another nine, the most severe penalty was a fine or compensation order; and for another 20, it was a community sentence. Taken together, these figures suggest that apart from the group sentenced to custody, the criminal careers of these young people were following a fairly modest course – more modest than might have been expected given their previous records, and, as we saw above, more modest than those of the comparison group, at least in terms of the risk of custody.

Table 6.9 Freagarrach: most severe sentence or order imposed by length of follow-up period

	Number of young people, by length of follow-up					
Most severe sentence or order	*6 months*	*12 months*	*2 years*	*3 years*	*4 years*	*Total of young people*
No further action	3	1	2	1	1	8
Admonished or police warning	0	0	1	2	0	3
Ongoing supervision	3	4	1	0	0	8
Supervision order (S.O.)	0	0	0	1	1	2
S.O. with residence requirement	0	0	4	0	1	5
Fine/compensation	0	1	2	3	4	10
Deferred sentence	2	3	2	0	0	7
Disqualified from driving	0	0	0	0	1	1
Probation or community service	0	2	4	8	8	22
Young Offenders Institution	0	3	4	3	7	17
Total	8	14	20	18	23	83

Another indicator of the seriousness of the young people's offending, and of what offences Freagarrach may in some cases have helped to prevent, comes from TRACE data on charges. This information was reasonably complete for the young people who came to Freagarrach during its first three years, though there were more gaps in the data for the third year group; in using the data it should also of course be borne in mind that TRACE counted charges (up to a maximum of five for each episode of offending), that the young people may have been innocent of some of the offences that led to charges, and that other charges were unlikely to lead to prosecution or other formal action. For the first three years, the total number of charges recorded against the young people in the 12-month period before they started at Freagarrach was 1,315; the comparable figure for the same group in the 12-month period after they had started at Freagarrach was 575, suggesting a total reduction of 740 charges (or almost 250 a year on average), or, in percentage terms, a reduction of 56 per cent. Given the proportions of different types of charge recorded on TRACE, the annual reduction in crimes of dishonesty was about 120, for miscellaneous offences it was about 50, for fire raising and vandalism it was about 40, and for violent offences it was about 30. These figures could be multiplied by five to give an estimate of the reduction over the period of the evaluation in these offence types, on the assumption of a constant annual rate of reduction.

It is likely, however, that this would overestimate Freagarrach's contribution to crime reduction, for four reasons: firstly, the fact that young people were attending Freagarrach may have led the police not to charge them when they would otherwise have done so; secondly, the TRACE figures for the first three years show a rate of reduction after the young people started at Freagarrach of, respectively, 28, 78, and 68 per cent, suggesting substantial year-on-year variation; thirdly, the gaps in TRACE data for the third year group mean that the figure of 68 per cent is based on an underestimate of the actual level of offending by this group; and fourthly, the TRACE figures are so different from those calculated from Scottish Criminal Records as to make it reasonable to suspect some problems with the data. Nevertheless, the TRACE figures confirm that a substantial reduction in the rate of offending by these young people did take place in the year after they started at Freagarrach, compared with the year before; and they provide an indication of what offences may have been prevented, and therefore of the types of victimisation that may have been avoided. The true extent of the reduction achieved in the first year after starting at Freagarrach is likely to be somewhere between the figure of 20 per cent suggested above and the 56 per cent suggested by the TRACE figures; in the following chapter, a minimum of 20 per cent and a maximum of 50 per cent are used in the analysis of the costs of Freagarrach and the savings it achieved.

Freagarrach worked with young people who in many cases had serious problems of social and personal adjustment, as well as the problems directly associated with offending. The project's first task was to engage the young people and, when possible, their families, in work that offered the possibility of positive change. When young people declined the project's offer of help, as a minority did, this was associated with worse outcomes in terms of subsequent offending than for the group of young people as a whole. As a corollary of this, there were indications that when both the young person and members of his or her family were engaged in working with the project, this was associated with positive outcomes in offending and other aspects of the young person's life, such as involvement in training and employment.

Freagarrach's impact on the development of criminal careers by the young people with whom it worked is hard to assess precisely, because different results emerge from different sources of data. There is no doubt, however, that the majority of the young people offended at a lower rate in the year after starting at the project than in the year before. The project thus contributed to a lower rate of offending by this group in the short term, and there were indications that over a two-year period young people who attended Freagarrach offended less seriously than those in the comparison group, who as a whole had been less persistent offenders in the year preceding the date from which records were examined. A longer term effect might also exist, since only 10 of the 41 young people on whom at least three years' follow-up data were available had been sentenced to custody, although all had been charged or convicted of some offence by that stage. In interpreting the results as indicating that Freagarrach 'worked' or did not, it is important to remember that the project dealt with almost all of the young people in central Scotland who were most at risk of long-term criminal careers; with such a group, total desistance from offending while still in young adulthood may be an unrealistic aspiration. A more reasonable measure of success is change in the rate and seriousness of offending, and on this measure Freagarrach can be judged to have succeeded with a majority of those with whom it worked. The implications of this and of other effects Freagarrach had on the young people's lives for cost savings are explored in the next chapter.

Chapter 7

Costs and Benefits

There are considerable problems in measuring the costs of crime and therefore the benefits of crime prevention, and it would be ridiculous to claim that it is, or can be, an exact science. No doubt partly because of this, work on the economics of criminal justice was slow to develop compared with studies of other areas of public expenditure, particularly health services (Knapp and Netten, 1997). During the period of the evaluations, however, governments began to show greater interest in the cost implications of criminal justice decisions (hence the publication of relevant material by the Scottish Office (1999)) and in the feasibility of measuring the costs of crime itself. While criminal justice system costs can be reasonably well estimated, it remains problematic to assign a cash value to the harm caused by the average crime of a particular type: ultimately, human suffering and distress cannot be quantified, although an attempt to quantify them was made by Brand and Price (2000) for the Home Office, which later published a quite radically revised set of estimates (Dubourg et al., 2005). The Home Office researchers included anticipatory costs such as those associated with security and insurance as well as consequential costs (arising principally from the effect on victims, loss of property, and health service costs) and costs to the criminal justice system. Their methods produce much higher costs for serious offences of violence, including sexual offences, than for property offences: most of the latter are costed by Dubourg et al. (2005: 7) at under £1,000 per offence, with burglary in a dwelling (housebreaking in Scotland) at £3,268 and theft of a motor vehicle at £4,138. In contrast, the average sexual offence is costed at £31,438 and the average case of serious wounding at £21,422 (but a common assault at only £1,440).

Because we cannot know what types of offences the young people who attended the projects might have committed had they not done so (even the estimate in Chapter 6 of the extent of reduction in violent offences attributable to Freagarrach necessarily conflates less and more serious offences), we have followed a narrower approach here, which counts only direct costs (from crimes committed) and savings (from crimes prevented) to the criminal justice system (and hence to government), rather than attempting to quantify costs and benefits to society at large, or the costs of the suffering of victims. This is the approach used by Karoly et al. (1998) in their work for the RAND Corporation on the crime-reducing effects of early childhood interventions, and on a smaller scale it was also suggested by the accountants Coopers and Lybrand (1997) in their work for the Prince's Trust in Scotland at the time of the evaluations. They offered two figures, the first, of about £2,700, representing the marginal cost of the average youth crime to society (that is, what society would save if the crime did not take place), the second, of £700, representing the marginal cost of a youth crime to the criminal justice system (what the system would save if the crime did not take place). The latter approach is the one adopted here: although it undoubtedly leaves some real costs out of account it has the advantage of being more closely related to demonstrable expenditure. Another analytic convention is also followed here, that of treating all criminal justice and related costs as net costs, disregarding the benefits that may arise from the employment of staff and the economic activity generated by the existence of a criminal justice system. No attempt has been made to adjust costs and savings for inflation, since the proportion of the total cost that is subject to inflationary price rises is not known, and efficiency savings may well have reduced some costs in the period under review. It should be noted that using the figure of £700 rather than £2,700 is more demanding of the projects in terms of the number of crimes they would need to prevent in order to show cost-effectiveness: a hypothetical project costing £50,000 a year would have to prevent about 20 crimes a year to produce a cost-saving if the average cost is taken as £2,700, but over 70 crimes using the figure of £700.

The Costs of CueTen

The total grant from the Scottish Office to Apex for the CueTen project was £588,162 over three years, or an average of £196,054 a year; the project's accounts showed a small amount of additional income, but this is disregarded here. Some of the costs related to establishing the project: in a full financial year after these start-up costs had been met the project cost £190,000. The bulk of expenditure (about 56 per cent) went on staff salaries and related costs; the next largest item in the budget was the rent for the premises. Since, over its lifetime, CueTen worked with, in effect, 93 young people (actually 86 individuals, since seven attended the project twice), the average cost per young person attending CueTen was £6,129 (counting running costs only, once the project was established). This figure can be compared with the 1997 estimate supplied by the Scottish Office Social Work Services Group of an average weekly cost per young person of about £1,800 for secure accommodation, and around £1,040 for placement for a week in a residential establishment with educational facilities. The Scottish Office (1999) estimated the cost of a probation order with no additional requirements at £1,450, the cost of a community service order at £1,320, and the cost of a six-month custodial sentence at £13,372, or just over £500 a week. The cost of a supervision order without a residential requirement is presumably similar to that of a probation order.

In fact, the real cost of providing a place for a young person at CueTen must have varied very widely around this average figure. Young people who completed the programme will obviously have cost more than those who attended only briefly; and those whose attendance was erratic and who constantly had to be chased will have cost more than the minority who were reliable attenders. The convening of a Children's Hearing was an additional cost, estimated by the Audit Commission (1996) as £880, which was incurred in those cases where a young person was excluded or ceased to attend, and the panel had to be informed, though it is impossible to say how many of these Hearings represented an extra cost (one that would not have been incurred had CueTen not existed). Similarly, it does not seem sensible to try to assign a monetary value to the contribution of other agencies to CueTen's work: although liaison with the project on the part of social workers and educational staff, and the contributions to its programme by the police and other agencies, certainly absorbed agency resources, and thus could be treated as involving opportunity costs, inter-agency communication is an inherent part of the work of staff in these agencies, not an additional burden. In fact, CueTen must have relieved both the Social Work and Education Departments of the costs that would have been incurred if social workers had been solely responsible for the young people's supervision, and teachers for their education. Thus, both costs and savings for these departments resulted from CueTen's existence.

The Costs of Freagarrach

The total cost of the Freagarrach Project over the period of the evaluation was £1,642,721, according to the project's own annual reports. The average annual cost, based on the four complete years, was £338,430; the average monthly cost for the entire period, treated as 58 months, was therefore £28,323. The bulk of the costs was contributed by central government, and the rest by Barnardo's Scotland and the local authorities, originally Central Regional Council, and from 1996 Clackmannanshire, Falkirk and Stirling. The support from the local authorities took the form of seconded staff and the provision of premises. Year on year variations in expenditure resulted from periods of staff absence and to a lesser extent from spending on equipment and the maintenance of premises; costs in the final two full years were only 4 per cent higher than in the first two full years.

During the period from the end of April 1995, when the first young person was recorded as having started at Freagarrach, the project worked with 106 young people, 15 of whom attended twice; in effect, therefore, the project worked with 121 young people, counting starts on the programme and places taken up, but disregarding the young people with whom Freagarrach staff worked informally, as described in Chapter 3. On this basis, the project worked on average with just over 24 young people in each year, giving an average cost for each young person of about £13,580, or an average weekly cost of about £350; as at CueTen, the actual costs will have varied greatly around this figure, depending on the length of time the young person spent at Freagarrach and the amount of work he or she generated. Using the Scottish Office figures given above in the discussion of CueTen, the cost can be calculated as equivalent to just under eight weeks in secure accommodation, about 13 weeks in a residential placement with educational facilities, and about six months in prison department custody. The average unit cost of Freagarrach was therefore closer to that usually associated with residential care or custody than to that associated with community-based measures like probation or community service orders (respectively about £1,450 and £1,300). This is not surprising, given the intensity of Freagarrach's involvement with young people and their families, but the unit cost was over twice that of the CueTen project, and the savings that Freagarrach would need to demonstrate, in terms of reducing offending and related costs, are correspondingly greater.

Apart from any impact it had on offending, Freagarrach could potentially deliver savings to other services in a number of ways: by reducing the use of secure accommodation and residential care, it could reduce costs for social work departments; by reducing the use of residential schooling and school exclusions, it could reduce costs for education departments; and by encouraging a reduced use of custody, it could reduce prison service costs. It could also produce some savings for social work departments insofar as its work relieved social work staff of the need to attend to some of the needs and demands of young people likely to be thought of as requiring intensive community supervision, but these possible savings are not considered here, since the requirement that social workers liaise with Freagarrach staff could be taken as an additional cost to social work departments: as with CueTen, Freagarrach's existence must have produced savings for social work departments (in supervision) as well as costs (in liaison). The possibility of savings from a reduced level of school exclusions is also not considered here, since, although the number of young people formally excluded fell during the period of the evaluation, very few returned to mainstream education, and the costs associated with providing some form of special education remained. The possible savings in the use of secure and residential care, and of custody, are considered below.

Cost-savings Achieved by CueTen

We suggested in Chapter 6 that in the period covered by the discussion of outcomes CueTen may have prevented 30 crimes. Over the full lifetime of the project, if the same rate of prevention was maintained, a total of 44 crimes will have been prevented (since the figure of 30 derives from work with 58 young people, and in all CueTen worked with 86; roughly, it prevented one crime on average for every two young people who attended). Using the average figure of £700 per crime as the marginal cost to the criminal justice system, the total saving can be estimated as £30,800. Even if the less demanding figure of a marginal cost to society of about £2,700 per youth crime were used, CueTen would not achieve a 'break-even' point on this measure; the 44 crimes prevented would have saved about £119,000, well below CueTen's cost over the three years of about £570,000.

There are, however, other savings which can be attributed to CueTen's work. If it prevented eight custodial sentences among 58 young people, and maintained this level of diversion from custody, it would have prevented 12 custodial sentences over three years. Using the Scottish Office figure for a six-month sentence, this would give a saving to the prison system of about £143,500 (treating the marginal cost of a six-month sentence as 90 per cent of the average cost). If the average length of a custodial sentence were shorter, the saving would of course be lower, and a figure of £100,000 might be a reasonable estimate of the cost saved by a reduced use of custody. Furthermore, CueTen, like any project providing intensive supervision, removed the need for residential care in a number of cases; from what is known of the backgrounds of the 58 young people discussed in the previous chapter, this number can be estimated as six. If each had spent three months in a residential establishment with educational facilities (not secure accommodation), the total cost would have been about £73,000 (using the figures cited above), and the marginal cost about £65,550 (calculating this on the same basis as for the saving to the prison service); over the life of the project, this rate of diversion from residential care would produce a saving of about £98,300. It is not plausible, however, to claim that CueTen produced substantial savings to the Education Department apart from those associated with residential schools, since the young people with whom it worked were not at school in any case. Savings would have been achieved had CueTen succeeded in enabling young people to move from special education to mainstream schools, but, as discussed above, this was not the case. The total cost-savings produced by CueTen over its lifetime would, therefore, be in the region of £229,000, compared with the cost of £570,000 for the project: it would therefore fall short of the break even point by around £341,000. The more generous estimate of the marginal cost of a crime would reduce this by about £90,000, but this would still leave a shortfall of some £251,000, a figure which could be regarded as a minimum estimate of the net cost of CueTen.

CueTen did not, then, deliver direct cost-savings to government over the three years of its life, but this is not, of course, to say that in cost-benefit terms it was less effective than other measures; relative to other measures – the mix of supervision, special education, residential care and custody which was delivered to the young people in the comparison group – it was probably reasonable value for money. There is also the possibility to be considered that it may have had much longer term effects which would eventually produce substantial cost-savings. If CueTen's work diverted three young people from an adult criminal career who would not otherwise have been diverted, as suggested in Chapter 6, and it is assumed that over the lifetime of the project it prevented one more criminal career from developing, the government would in time be spared the cost of four criminal careers. Greenwood et al. (1998: 57) estimate the criminal justice costs of the criminal career of a high rate offender as about $75,700 at 1993 prices (and as nearly double this with full implementation in California of the 'three strikes and you're out' legislation). Their definition of a high rate offender is simply one who commits more than the average number of offences for the known population of offenders; since CueTen worked with some of the worst risk cases among the juvenile offender population of Fife, it is reasonable to assume that any criminal careers prevented would have been at the top end of the distribution. The criminal justice system cost of such a criminal career would, on the basis of the figures given by the Scottish Office (1998) be closer to £100,000 than the roughly £50,000 suggested by Greenwood and his colleagues (assuming, for example, that such a career would entail 20 court appearances resulting in conviction and a total of two years spent in custody, and also assuming Scottish rather than Californian sentencing practices). The cost-saving achieved by the prevention of four criminal careers would therefore be about £400,000, spread over (say) ten to 12 years, taking this as the length of a serious criminal career (Farrington, 1992). The cost benefits would, of course be much greater if the total cost of crimes to society as a whole were considered, and not merely the direct cost savings to the criminal justice system.

The point of this account is not to claim definitely that CueTen prevented the development of four criminal careers – the evidence is only suggestive, and in any case the young people concerned, while they were certainly at high risk according to the best-established predictors, may have been 'false positives'. It is, rather, to illustrate the importance for policy on crime reduction to take account of possible long-term as well as immediate cost-savings; early intervention projects may not show definite cost savings or benefits for 15 years or more (Karoly et al., 1998). If the above analysis is correct, however, CueTen may have delivered long-term cost savings, albeit modest ones, which an exclusive focus on short-term results would not reveal.

Cost-savings Achieved by Freagarrach

The senior staff who were interviewed about their experience of Freagarrach believed that the project might well have prevented an increase in the use of residential care for the relevant age group, but were unable to quantify the extent of this saving. In order to obtain a clearer view of possible savings in this area, the circumstances of each of the young people at the time of their arrival at Freagarrach were examined and discussed with project staff, with a focus on the part the project had played in diverting the young people from care or custody, shortening the time they spent in care, or delaying their entry into the care or custodial systems. This investigation took place at the end of 1999 and covered 94 young people.

Apart from the young people for whom, by virtue of their age, custody rather than care was the threat, 12 young people were identified for whom care was not an issue; in these cases, therefore, no saving had been achieved by attendance at Freagarrach. In another 42 cases it was not possible to identify any difference in outcome, in respect of the use of care or custody, that resulted from Freagarrach's intervention. These cases included the nine young people who never engaged with the project; in other cases, the young person had either remained in some form of official care or entered it after or during his or her time at Freagarrach; and in a few others, the young person had received a custodial sentence despite the project's efforts. In some cases, not enough information was available to make a judgement. It should be noted that the project staff were not dogmatically opposed to the use of residential resources; in a few cases, they believed that residential school, for example, was in the young person's best interests, or that secure accommodation was the only realistic option. There is no evidence, however, that attendance at Freagarrach ever led to, or even increased the likelihood of, entry into care; a reduction in the use of residential care was a key aim of the project from the start, and one to which the staff were strongly committed; and the project's success in maintaining a focus on its original target group meant that the potential problem of net-widening never materialised. The theoretical possibility that Freagarrach increased the use of care (and therefore increased costs) can be discounted.

Of the remaining 40 young people, we identified 28[1] as cases where Freagarrach's involvement had had an impact on the young person's experience of care, and 12

---

1   This figure is lower than the project staff's own original estimate of 34, given in the previous chapter.

where it had affected the use of custody. Sometimes the evidence of this impact was direct and obvious, as when a Children's Panel had indicated that it was considering secure accommodation, or a Sheriff said that had it not been for Freagarrach the young person would have been sent to custody. In other cases, Freagarrach had been used specifically as a means of helping the young person to leave care and begin his or her reintegration into family and community. For some young people, however, Freagarrach's impact had to be inferred from knowledge of their circumstances at the time of their arrival at Freagarrach, and of the thinking at the time of social workers and others about what the available options were.

In 12 cases, it was judged that the young person would have gone to, or spent longer at, a residential school had it not been for Freagarrach's intervention. The estimated number of months at residential school 'saved' by Freagarrach ranged from six to 24 months, and totalled 150. The cost of providing residential education for this period would be about £660,000, but since the alternative made possible by Freagarrach involved foster care for at least one of these young people, and it was rare for them to return to mainstream education, the net saving will have been rather less than this: if 10 per cent is discounted to allow for these factors, and, following the procedure of Greenwood et al. (1998), a further 10 per cent is deducted to allow for the fact that some costs are fixed and thus to produce the marginal cost saving (90 per cent of the average cost), the net saving on residential education can be estimated as £528,000. For four young people, Freagarrach was judged to have removed the need for secure accommodation; on the assumption that the average length of stay in secure conditions would have been six months (a conservative assumption in the light of the time spent in secure accommodation by the young people at Freagarrach who had some experience of it), the saving achieved would be £187,200. On the basis, again, of discounts of 10 per cent to allow for alternative care arrangements and the marginal cost saving, the net saving can be set at £150,000. For another 12 young people, Freagarrach removed or curtailed the need for some other form of residential care; the average length of residence for those cases on which an estimate could be made was 12 months, giving a total period of care avoided of 144 months. On the assumption that the average cost of accommodation in a children's home is half that of residential education, the saving in respect of these young people can be estimated as £325,000. Since these young people did not generally receive any other form of substitute care, the marginal cost saving (90 per cent) can be treated as the net amount saved, giving a saving of £292,500. Overall, therefore, during the period of the evaluation Freagarrach probably enabled a net saving in the use of various kinds of residential care of just under £1 million, representing an average annual saving of about £202,000.

Savings were also estimated from the reduction in the use of prison department custody resulting from Freagarrach's involvement. An effect – diversion from custody or delaying of the first custodial sentence – was identified for 12 young people; this estimate is close to that arrived at in Chapter 6 through the two-year analysis of the use of custody for the Freagarrach group and the comparison group. On the assumption that the custodial sentences avoided would have been short – say, leading to an average of three months actually in custody – the saving in the use of custody would amount to about £78,000; the net amount saved can be treated as £70,000, discounting only 10 per cent to give the marginal cost saving, since these young people were not placed in any other kind of official accommodation. This figure brings the total estimated saving in a reduced use of custody and care to about £1,040,000, an average annual saving of about £217,000; the net cost of Freagarrach over the period of the evaluation would then be just over £600,000, or about £125,000 a year. It should be noted that the estimate for Freagarrach's effect on the use of custody refers only to the two-year period after young people started attending the project; there were indications, discussed in Chapter 6, that the use of custody for young people who had been at Freagarrach remained lower than might have been expected over a longer period, so savings from a reduced use of custody may well have been greater in the long term. Short-term savings on custody, however, are likely to be modest compared with savings on care, which, in view of the age of the young people at Freagarrach, are inherently short – to medium-term. As Freagarrach dealt with more young people towards the upper end of its target age range as time went on, the savings from a reduced use of care must have declined over the period of the evaluation.

The other main source of possible savings from Freagarrach is of course the prevention of crimes. The problems of estimating how many crimes Freagarrach may have helped to prevent were discussed in Chapter 6, where we argued that a reasonable minimum figure for the percentage reduction in offending in the year following the young people's arrival at Freagarrach was 20 per cent; this took account of the shortcomings of Scottish Criminal Records data as well as of the need to disregard some convictions as false positives in assessing the effectiveness of community-based measures. The discussion also noted how different estimates could be reached if the TRACE data were used; TRACE suggested a percentage reduction of 56 per cent, but because of limitations in the coverage of TRACE it was suggested that a reasonable maximum figure was a reduction of 50 per cent. TRACE provides a better measure of offending by juveniles than Scottish Criminal Records, since it includes almost all charges (including those of which the young people may have been innocent); but it is inherently limited to juvenile offending, and provides no information on young people who were 16 at the time they started at Freagarrach.

The minimum estimate of a 20 per cent reduction in the number of crimes committed by young people in the year after they started at Freagarrach compared with the year before, on the basis of charges recorded in TRACE, produces an annual figure of 90; at an average marginal cost of £700, the annual saving would be £63,000, and the total saving to 31 March 2000 would be about £302,000. The 90 crimes would typically consist of 45 offences of dishonesty, 19 'miscellaneous' offences, 15 offences of vandalism or fire-raising, and 11 violent offences. On the maximum estimate of Freagarrach's short-term crime reduction effect, the annual figure would be 226, giving a saving of £158,200, and a total saving over the whole period of about £759,000. The figure of 226 would be made up in the same proportions as for the lower estimate, giving 113 offences of dishonesty, 47 miscellaneous offences, 38 offences of vandalism or fire-raising, and 28 violent offences. On the lower estimate, the net cost of Freagarrach over the period of the evaluation – the extent to which it did not deliver a direct cost-saving – would be about £300,000; on the higher estimate, Freagarrach would have contributed a direct saving to the criminal justice and social work services of about £160,000. If the figure of £2,700 were used as the average cost to society of a youth crime, Freagarrach would have saved about £240,000 annually on the lower estimate, and about £610,000 annually on the higher. On the least generous estimate, then, the annual net cost of Freagarrach was just over £60,000, taking account of the savings to the criminal justice system through the reduction of offending by the young people with whom it worked; on the most generous estimate (but still counting only direct costs and savings), it produced a net annual saving of about £33,300. The arbitrary procedure of splitting the difference gives an annual net cost of £13,350. On any estimate of its crime reduction effect, however, Freagarrach helped bring about a substantial saving in the total social costs of crime: for the entire period, this saving was, on the lower estimate, over £1 million, on the higher estimate, just under £3 million.

These figures take account only of short-term savings, resulting from Freagarrach's immediate impact on the young people's offending and on the use of other types of care or punishment. Although the exercise inevitably entails some speculation, it is possible to estimate, as we did for CueTen, the longer-term savings Freagarrach may have produced by diverting young people from criminal careers. The tables in Chapter 6, and the comparison of the proportions of the Freagarrach group and the comparison group sentenced to custody, provide a basis for estimating the extent to which this type of diversion was achieved. Only ten of the 41 young people with at least three years' follow-up data had been sentenced to custody; and 25 of them – 13 of the three-year and 12 of the four-year group – had received a sentence or other disposal in court or at a Children's Hearing on fewer than six occasions. Given that these young people were on all established measures among those most at risk of developing a long-term criminal career, these figures suggest that Freagarrach may have had a long-term effect that helped to divert some of them from continued high-rate offending. As we saw, Greenwood et al. (1998) estimate the cost to the criminal justice system of a criminal career as roughly £50,000, but their definition of 'career' is conservative, and the young people at Freagarrach threatened to go on to criminal careers that were almost exclusively at the top end of the distribution of career types, so, as with CueTen, the figure of £100,000 seems a more plausible estimate of the cost of the kind of criminal career that Freagarrach may have prevented. The data on court appearances and custodial sentencing suggest that Freagarrach may have helped to divert about half of the young people it worked with from criminal careers; this would produce a total saving of about £4.8 million from diversion of the group of young people on whom at least six months' data are available, realised over a period of 10–12 years (Farrington, 1992). A more cautious view of the results might still lead to the conclusion that Freagarrach had a diversionary effect on about a quarter of the young people it worked with (twelve out of the 41 young people in the three-and four-year groups had been in court or before a Hearing on fewer than three occasions), but this would still produce a direct saving of about £2.4 million. Again, these figures are based on cost savings to the criminal justice system, and not to society as a whole.

There is no doubt that, compared with most community-based services for juvenile offenders, Freagarrach was an expensive project. Its costs, however, were a direct product of the intensity of work that it provided, and of the fact that it worked with many young people over substantial periods of time. The unit cost (the average cost of a young person's attendance at Freagarrach) was higher than had been originally planned, because Freagarrach worked with fewer young people than had been envisaged; this was inevitable, given the highly individualised style of work the project staff developed, and the gravity of the needs and problems of many of the young people who attended it. As was shown in Chapter 3, there is no evidence that there was a large population of young people who should have come to Freagarrach but were denied the opportunity to do so.

In considering whether Freagarrach delivered value for money, it is important to be clear about the criteria by which this should be judged. There is an understandable tendency for agencies that support such a project to look for immediate and readily identifiable short-term savings. The most obvious way in which Freagarrach might have done this is by reducing the need for other, more expensive services – essentially, those involving some form of residential care. Although there are strong indications that Freagarrach did remove or curtail the need to use such services for a substantial minority of the young people with whom it worked, its net cost over the period of the evaluation was still about £680,000 – or about £600,000 if savings in the use of prison custody are included. These figures take no account, however, of the savings Freagarrach may have produced through reducing, in the short term, the rate of offending among the young people who attended it. If these less apparent cost savings (to the Children's Hearing System, the police and prosecution services, local authority services, and the courts) are taken into account, Freagarrach's net cost over the whole period was (on the least generous estimate of its crime reduction effect) about £300,000; and on the most generous sensible estimate, it produced a net saving of about £160,000. Thus, even without considering the broader social costs of crime, and disregarding the long-term benefits from diversion of young people from adult criminal careers, Freagarrach's net costs were much lower than the headline figure of the project's expenditure would suggest. It is doubtful, to say the least, that the savings Freagarrach made possible, and the benefits that flowed from its impact on the offending rate of the most persistent juvenile offenders in central Scotland, could have been achieved with an initial outlay much lower than the £1.64 million spent on Freagarrach.

Conclusions

The approach taken in this chapter to the analysis of the projects' costs and savings has been cautious, in that it has mainly focused only on the most direct costs of crimes, those that are reflected in the work of the Children's Hearing and criminal justice systems. A more speculative approach that attempted to calculate the costs of crime to society at large, and to quantify the harm to victims of crimes of different types, would have produced a more generous account, certainly in the case of Freagarrach, of the savings and benefits that resulted for society through the prevention of crimes. As well as leaving victims out of the equation, the calculation of costs and savings or benefits on this narrow basis also leaves out of account the real but unquantifiable benefits to young offenders and their families, but we hope that these have been identified clearly enough in earlier chapters. It is inevitable and right that when public money has been spent on projects like CueTen and Freagarrach there should be some public accounting of whether the money was well spent, but there are aspects of the projects' work, as there are aspects of human experience, that cannot be quantified in this way, and in the concluding chapter we attempt a more inclusive evaluation of the projects, and suggest what lessons might be drawn from their experiences.

Chapter 8

An Overall Evaluation of the Projects

CueTen

The origins of the two projects were linked, since CueTen was funded as a result of the Scottish Office initiative that led to the establishment of Freagarrach. Apex Scotland's part in a bid for project funding aroused the interest of Scottish Office civil servants to the point where they invited a second bid, from Apex acting on its own. The bid promised something different and innovative, and the fact that these were attractive qualities to the civil servants is indicative of the policy context of the time: not only was the Scottish Office committed to a serious attempt to develop community-based resources for persistent juvenile offenders, it was prepared to take a risk in supporting an organisation that had no experience of work with juveniles, and proposed an approach to working with them that was ambitious and untested. The Scottish Office staff were taken by Apex's style as well as by the content of the programme it offered: this looked like an organisation that was action-orientated, practical, capable of getting things done, and less cerebral and introspective than the social work organisations with which the civil servants were accustomed to deal. Apex promised a quick translation of ideas into reality, with a minimum of bureaucracy and a commitment to practical action. Instead of the usual mix of group work and counselling (more or less what, on paper, Freagarrach offered), Apex offered a training curriculum that was an adaptation of its work with adult offenders, with a focus on the development of practical skills and attitudes favourable to success in the labour market. The Scottish Office decided to provide funding for three years to allow these ideas to be worked out in practice, and Apex used the funding to establish the CueTen project on an industrial estate in the former New Town of Glenrothes, with the whole of Fife as its catchment area. Fife was chosen because Apex already had a presence there, and because the reorganisation of local government in 1996 would have relatively little impact there.

The CueTen project was, in line with the expectations of the Scottish Office, established quickly, but there were penalties associated with its rapid appearance on the scene. Fife had a recent history of tension between the Social Work and Education Departments over alleged failures of consultation, and CueTen had to begin work in an environment of high sensitivity to the possibility of more such failures. For at least the first two years of CueTen's existence, there were complaints from senior staff, particularly in the Education Department, that it had been set up without adequate consultation and preparation. Basic practical questions that should have been settled from the outset, such as who should pay for the transport of young people to the project, were not resolved until much later; and the idea of a local inter-agency management group for the project took a long time to materialise.

Perhaps more crucially, the number of young people in Fife who could reasonably be defined as persistent juvenile offenders, even on the fairly relaxed definition of persistence agreed between CueTen and social work staff, turned out to be smaller than the original plans had envisaged. CueTen worked with about two-thirds of the eligible young people in Fife during its three years, and very rarely strayed from its intended target group; but the staff were never in a position to be selective about which young people they accepted, which meant that some of the young people who were referred had a very low level of commitment to the project, and little interest in making a success of their time there. The problem of weak motivation and low expectations was sometimes aggravated, or at least not alleviated, by the rather minimalist messages social workers gave young people about what they could expect at CueTen, and the importance of their regular attendance there.

The problems of erratic and unwilling attendance and participation that arose from lack of commitment were compounded by the nature of the CueTen programme. It set out to deliver a well defined curriculum over an initial period of 13 weeks, followed by a period of more individual work designed to prepare the young people for the final block of work experience or introductory training. The whole programme lasted for 26 weeks, a long time in the life of any young person, and a seriously long time for young people who had long ceased to attend school regularly, as was the case with most of those who came to CueTen. The programme proved too ambitious and demanding for many of the young people; at the end of the research period, just over half, 44 out of 80, of those who attended the project had completed the first 13-week block of the programme, and 29 out of a possible 72 had finished, or virtually finished, the whole programme. Twenty-six young people left of their own accord or as a result of circumstances in their lives unconnected with CueTen, and another 20 were excluded for violent or otherwise unacceptable behaviour. (In summary, of the 80, 29 completed the programme, 26 left, 20 were excluded, and five were still attending at the end of the research.) The modest completion rate is not surprising in view of the demands of the programme and the nature of the client group, but the CueTen staff were constantly distracted from work on the formal programme by the need to check reasons for absence.

The staff were also surprised, early in the life of the project, by the sheer weight of problems many of these young people brought with them to the project. Apex's experience and traditions had not prepared the staff to deal with the emotional, attitudinal and behavioural difficulties displayed by this group of young people, as a consequence of the experience of loss, deprivation, rejection and abuse which many of them, in common with persistent offenders in general, had suffered. The actual delivery of the CueTen programme, therefore, was never the orderly and rational process that had been set down at the beginning; the staff continually had to adapt, negotiate, and modify their plans, and spent a great deal more time in individual work than they had expected. They showed skill and perseverance in adjusting their work to the circumstances that confronted them, but their lack of access to the young people's families limited the amount of change they could expect to achieve at the individual level, since family relationships were in many cases the major source of the young people's disturbance and unhappiness. A different staff group, for instance one in which social work skills and experience were more strongly represented, would not have needed to embark on such a steep learning curve; but the problems inherent in CueTen's design – a long formal curriculum and a lack of opportunity to work on family relationships – would have remained.

Everyday life at CueTen was often fraught. The problems staff found in the basic management of the young people meant that they had little time for the more outward-looking, developmental work which was crucial to CueTen's (and Apex's) commitment to integrating the young offenders with the wider community. One aspect of the initial scheme, that the young people at CueTen should have access to a network of young people in employment locally, who would support them in the transition to the world of work, never materialised. Links with employers were never as fully developed as the staff would have wished, and were not made easier to establish by the tendency of some young people to carry their aggressive and anti-social behaviour into places of work and education. Staff morale was not helped by their sense that the particular problems of working with this group of young people were not appreciated by their managers in Apex, and by the anxiety about future employment that some staff felt towards the end of the project's period of funding.

The picture was not, however, unrelievedly bleak. There is no doubt that CueTen helped some young people to acquire new knowledge and skills, and a new sense of self-belief, and that this could be associated with a reduced rate of offending. The short-term outcomes in terms of reconvictions for all but four of the group who completed the programme were moderately encouraging, and even when those who left or were excluded are counted, there were signs that the CueTen group had slightly better prospects of avoiding a long-term criminal career than the comparison group of 39 young people, broadly similar in terms of their offending, who for various reasons did not attend CueTen. While CueTen did not demonstrate direct cost-savings during its lifetime, it may have contributed to substantial savings in the longer term; and it was probably slightly more cost-effective than the range of interventions to which the comparison group was subject. In addition, as an experimental project from which it was hoped that something could be learned, CueTen provided some potentially important messages for policy.

Firstly, CueTen was an example of a specialist project that was not well embedded in the network of agencies on which it depended not only for referrals but for support and understanding. Many, though not all, of the problems the project encountered arose from its failure to be fully accepted, at least until late in its life, by the statutory agencies in Fife, as a valid and integral part of the services available locally for young offenders. CueTen never received as much information as the staff felt would have been useful from social workers or from the police; some social workers were quite ready to use it as little more than a dumping-ground for their most intractable cases; there were enduring sources of irritation between CueTen and the Education Department, not only over the costs of transport but over the relationship between CueTen's programme and the school curriculum which, notionally, the young people were still supposed to be following; and the broad-based local steering group which was needed to promote a sense of commitment and ownership across the agencies was not established until the project's final year. More careful consultation at the initial stage of setting up the project would have at least reduced the impact of such deficiencies in communication and support, and provided a basis for continuing joint review of progress, the identification of common problems, and shared work on adapting and developing the project. Had such careful consultation taken place, indeed, it is likely that CueTen would have been a substantially different project.

Secondly, there was a strong positive relationship between successful completion of the CueTen programme and lower rates of known offending in the 12 months prior to starting it – hardly a surprising finding. It could be used, of course, to argue that a programme like CueTen should be targeted at this group – relatively infrequent or minor young offenders who are to some degree alienated from the formal education system. It is not clear, however, that this would be a sensible use of resources, since it would entail the provision of a relatively expensive specialist service, with crime reduction aims, to a group unlikely in any case to develop serious criminal careers. There would also be the danger that such a project might do more harm through negative labelling and disruption of normal development (Cleaver, 1991; Braithwaite, 1999) than it did good through the provision of new skills and knowledge; and it would contravene the 'risk principle' that intensity of intervention should be proportional to likelihood of reoffending (Andrews, 1995). A more fruitful conclusion to be drawn from the finding is that the CueTen programme was most likely to succeed with young people with reasonably well developed social skills and coping capacities, and who were not excessively burdened by stresses arising from domestic unhappiness, or deeply enmeshed in subcultures of petty crime or substance abuse. That is, the rational, cognitive approach of CueTen is generally only going to be effective with young people who have achieved the level of maturity and social adjustment required to sit attentively through a long and complex curriculum, to see the point of it in terms of their own lives and prospects, and to use their learning in making the transition to the adult world of work and its disciplines and demands. The CueTen staff could not, and should not have been expected to, act as individual counsellors on a wide range of personal difficulties, let alone as family therapists.

Thirdly, the young people who attended CueTen, as well as social workers and teachers, felt that the programme made most sense when it was conceived exactly in this way, as providing a bridge between school and employment or further education, or even from childhood to near adult status. It made much less sense when it was to be followed by a return to school, and there were in fact no cases in which a young person went back to school without difficulty after attending CueTen; the most common outcome in these cases was that the young person never went back.

This experience, combined with the point about the qualities required if young people are to cope with a programme like CueTen's, suggests a possible way of thinking about the place of such a project in the range of services. This would be a place familiar to Apex from its other work – a place of transition. One can imagine, for example, that a programme like CueTen's might be useful in preparing young people for discharge from a Young Offenders Institution, or perhaps for leaving long-term residential care. In both these settings, attendance would be voluntary, so that only the well-motivated and interested would participate; and attendance throughout the programme, while desirable, would not be a requirement. The experience of CueTen also suggests that such a programme could provide valuable support for young people with a history of persistent offending as juveniles who have reached the age when they will not be expected to return to school, so that they are moving forwards in the life-course rather than backwards, and who have already resolved some of the problems characteristic of many of the young people who attended CueTen. A programme of this kind might serve as a bridge into participation in the labour market and community life for young people who have already benefited from a more conventionally therapeutic form of intervention, to the point where problems in family relationships have either become manageable or been transcended with a move to independent living, problems such as drug or alcohol abuse have been controlled, and delinquent subcultures have lost some of their appeal. As in the institutional setting, attendance would be voluntary (though it could also be authoritatively encouraged). This was exactly the role envisaged for Apex's unfortunately short-lived project in Stirling in relation to the Freagarrach Project, and it is to be hoped that another opportunity will arise to test the feasibility of the CueTen model of practice in this context. In the light of the first of these concluding points, any renewed attempt to provide such a service should start with extensive consultation with relevant local constituencies, and proceed only once they have committed themselves to its support.

Freagarrach

In one of the most obvious and important contrasts between its situation and CueTen's, Freagarrach benefited from the outset from being embedded in a local strategy that brought the various agencies concerned with juvenile offending together with a common sense of purpose. Originally a product of a police initiative, the strategy was agreed by key staff in the relevant departments of Central Regional Council, the Reporter's Service, and Barnardo's Scotland, which had an established presence in the area and a high level of credibility with relevant audiences. The disaggregation of Central Region, and the changes of personnel associated with it, meant that the principle of a joint strategy, its direction and purpose, and the structures and procedures that were needed to give it practical effect all had to be renegotiated; in this process, the continuity provided by the police and by Barnardo's was crucial. Inter-agency and cross-authority commitment to the strategy, and to Freagarrach, was maintained until early in 2000, when Clackmannanshire withdrew its financial support.

The strategy was ambitious and wide-ranging, and was not successfully implemented in all respects: resources never allowed for the development of some of the services for young people that had been envisaged, such as a common information system for all the participating agencies, an electronically accessible inventory of youth resources, and a mentoring system. Nevertheless, the fact that there was a common strategy with authoritative support benefited Freagarrach by conveying the message to local authority staff – importantly, in the social work and education services – and to Reporters and Children's Panel members that this was a resource to be valued and supported. At the level of day-to-day practice, the Freagarrach staff also benefited from the willingness of the police to share information with them on the young people who were at any time the most persistent juvenile offenders in central Scotland. This allowed the project to avoid the potential problem of net-widening and retain as its target group those who were, on the strongest evidence available, the most persistent offenders in the 12–16 – later 12–18 – age group; it also allowed the staff to demonstrate that this was the case. The difficulties that can be predicted to arise in inter-agency working duly arose (Pearson et al., 1992), but the will to resolve them, and the structures that made their resolution possible, remained largely intact.

Freagarrach's status as 'the tip of the iceberg,' as an enthusiast for the strategy described it, helped it to avoid many of the problems that are often encountered by projects that are not as well integrated into a coherent local strategy: problems such as isolation, insufficient knowledge and interest on the part of field social workers, lack of referrals, and pressure to accept inappropriate cases. The project's staff were not thereby relieved of the need to work at establishing and maintaining credibility and awareness, but their task was undoubtedly made easier by the high-level support Freagarrach enjoyed. While exact replication of any project is impossible (Tilley, 1993), it is plausible to claim, on the basis of the Freagarrach experience, that as a matter of principle a specialist project should be conceived not as a stand-alone enterprise but as one part of a broader programmatic effort, and that this principle should inform all developments of such projects in future, certainly within the field of crime reduction (King, 1988), and perhaps in relation to any social problem. The need for coherent inter-agency strategies and partnerships on youth crime was recognised in statute in England and Wales in the 1998 Crime and Disorder Act, and was given practical expression in the form of (among other things) Youth Offending Teams; it was also stressed in the recommendations of the Youth Crime Review in Scotland, which reported in the summer of 2000, and led to the establishment of multi-agency Youth Justice Teams.[1] The experience of Freagarrach, and of those in central Scotland who persisted with the principle of partnership, provides a positive example from which others interested in policy coherence, and in making a success of multi-agency working, can draw encouragement and hope.

The other main distinguishing characteristic of Freagarrach was the quality of its direct work with the young people and, when possible, their families: on all recognised criteria the standard of practice was exceptionally high. This was not simply because the staff consciously worked in ways that evidence suggests are most likely to be effective in helping offenders change, though this was certainly the case; it is quite possible to follow the canons of effectiveness and still provide a service that is not perceived as helpful and changes nothing – for example, if a programme is delivered in an alienating, punitive or merely didactic style. The Freagarrach staff, in contrast, succeeded in conveying a sense of care and warmth even as they indicated what the boundaries of acceptable behaviour were – a claim based on observation of practice and the testimony of many young people and members of their families. One of the classics of systematic evaluative research on the effectiveness of social work and similar forms of intervention (Truax and Carkhuff, 1967) can be read as

---

1   Thirty-two teams were established to cover the whole of Scotland, with a membership typically including representatives from the following agencies: social work, education, housing, leisure and recreation, police, health, Children's Hearings, procurator fiscal's department, courts, prisons, and the voluntary sector (Scottish Executive, 2002).

saying that the content of the theories and methods used by practitioners matters less than the style in which these are delivered in practice; almost, that good practitioners are also good people. Subsequent research has shown that content does matter in work with offenders (Mc Guire, 1995); but this should not obscure the basic truth that style also matters, and that acceptance, empathy and warmth are also associated with success in helping people change. These were qualities in the Freagarrach staff that were frequently mentioned, though not in these words, by young people and members of their families, and seen by them as essential elements of their experience of Freagarrach. For some of the young people, the project may have been the first setting in which they felt that their most basic needs – for care, comfort and even physical nourishment – were adequately recognised and met.

There were features of Freagarrach's work that could be criticised, as, at various times, the staff themselves recognised. It was sometimes not clear either to the evaluators or the staff which young people ought actually to be counted as attending the project: some were still counted although they were barely in contact, others, who had officially left, were still being seen frequently. It was sometimes difficult for the staff to 'let go' of young people, just as it was difficult for some young people to move on. The aspiration that the staff had to break down inter-professional barriers and undertake more joint work with staff from the police and other agencies remained more an aspiration and less of a reality than they themselves would have wished. The staff's sense that other agencies were under pressure of work, so that it was easier to do things themselves than to try to engage a specialist service as an additional resource (for example on drug counselling), may at times have stretched their expertise to its limits. Informed observers believed, however, that even in specialist fields it was likely that the Freagarrach staff provided a better service than was realistically available elsewhere: the staff group was itself multi-disciplinary, as a matter of policy, and, as a result of the practice of seconding staff from local authorities (another benefit of partnership), its members had the security of employment that enables continuity and an undistracted focus on the tasks in hand.

Freagarrach's main focus was on offending, and the staff used the cognitive-behavioural approach recommended by research on effectiveness to help the young people think more clearly about the damage they were doing to themselves and others by their offences, but they also recognised that a focus on cognition – on thinking – needed to be complemented by a concern with emotion – with how the young people felt. The project worked with a population that consisted not only of many of the most persistent juvenile offenders in the region but of some of the most emotionally scarred. The staff themselves were surprised by the frequency with which experiences of loss, abandonment and rejection featured in the lives of the young people with whom they worked. These experiences had often left a legacy of anger, hostility, resentment and aggression, powerful emotions that had to be acknowledged if young people were to be successfully engaged in working towards change. The care and respect shown by the staff towards the young people were therefore not optional extras, let alone the sentimental expression of a misplaced concern to understand rather than condemn: they were essential ingredients in the process of engendering the hope that positive change was possible, and in freeing young people to feel emotions other than the hostility and anger that are the product of rejection and disrespect (Scheff, 1997).

These characteristics of the young people need to be borne in mind, along with the seriousness and persistence of their offending before they came to Freagarrach, in interpreting their subsequent offending histories. It would not be realistic, for many of these young people, to expect that any professional intervention would produce complete desistance from offending, though there were instances of young people whose offending declined dramatically both in frequency and seriousness. It would be possible, for example, to treat the finding that it was rare for young people to remain free of further convictions in a two-year period from the start of their attendance at Freagarrach as a disappointing result, but this would be to underestimate the depth of their involvement in offending before they started, and the strength of the forces – personal, relational, and subcultural – that had to be overcome for offending to cease, or even diminish. The burden of the argument about Freagarrach in Chapter 6 was rather that the project should be judged by evidence of its impact on offence seriousness and frequency, and that, on these more realistic measures, the project could demonstrate an impressive degree of success. Given the presence in Freagarrach of the elements of practice repeatedly shown to be associated with good results in work with offenders, it would be surprising if it had been otherwise. Again, if a realistic view is taken of the kind of cost savings Freagarrach could be expected to deliver, the results reported in Chapter 7 will be interpreted as showing that, although at first sight an expensive project which could be dismissed as an extravagance, Freagarrach can claim to have delivered short-term savings that made its net costs much lower than they might appear simply from looking at expenditure on the project since 1995.

The lessons to be learned from the evaluation of Freagarrach are therefore mainly positive ones. The most important are probably i) that projects of this kind are much more likely to succeed when they are established as one element of a coherent inter-agency strategy, and based on a serious effort to determine the scale of the target problem, and ii) that practice of the quality needed to make a difference requires a well-trained and supported staff team, aware of the findings of effectiveness research and willing to put them into practice while maintaining an attitude of respect for and acceptance of young people. The ability of the Freagarrach staff to convey these human qualities while remaining clear that the young people's offending was harmful and unacceptable seems to have been much more effective in gaining a positive response from most of those it worked with than any amount of attempted compulsion would have been. Although the exact circumstances of Freagarrach's establishment and development will never be precisely replicated, the project, viewed in the context of the local strategy on young people in trouble, could usefully become a model for policy and practice elsewhere. Anyone considering a similar development should, however, remember that the initial expenditure will inevitably look high, that high quality staff (working in a reasonable physical environment) are essential, and are unlikely to be available – or to work to their full capacity – without security of employment, and that partnership across agency boundaries requires sustained practical commitment, not merely rhetorical flourishes.

Conclusions

We hope by now to have justified the claim in the Introduction that the evaluation of two projects in Scotland in the last years of the twentieth century contains messages with more general resonance and value for anyone interested in what does and does not work with persistent juvenile offenders. Some of the messages are relatively uncontroversial: for example that context matters, or that programmes need to be adaptable and flexible enough to meet a range of needs and problems, and different aptitudes and approaches to learning. Others may seem plausible to the research community, or at least some members of it, while appearing much less so to policy-makers and the researchers most closely associated with them: for example, that there may be no need for a court order, backed by threats of punishment for non-compliance, in order to achieve a high level of participation; or that an approach that expresses care, concern and respect may be more effective than one based on suspicion, surveillance and (attempted) control. In the twenty-first century, the main thrust of policy on young offenders in England and Wales, and – even if less consistently – in Scotland, has been towards greater intensity of supervision, with more requirements and prohibitions, and a more complicated legal apparatus to enforce it: think of Intensive Supervision and Surveillance Programmes, electronic tagging, curfews, and so on. The success – which is what we have argued it is – of Freagarrach was and is based on very different principles, including those of voluntarism and welfare, on which the Children's Hearings System was founded. The findings from Freagarrach, we have suggested, support rather than contradict the main lines of research on effectiveness over the past decade, particularly but not only the more recent work which has reasserted the importance of the quality of the relationship between helper and helped (summarised with a Scottish emphasis in McNeill (2006)). What they do contradict is the politically fashionable view that the only way to enhance the effectiveness of community supervision is through tighter controls and more rigorous enforcement. If this book helps to strengthen the challenge to that view it will have achieved perhaps its most important purpose.

Bibliography

Andrews, D. (1995) 'The Psychology of Criminal Conduct and Effective Treatment' in *What Works: Reducing Reoffending*, McGuire, J. (ed.) (Chichester: John Wiley).

Andrews, D.A., Keissling, J.J., Robinson, D. and Michus, S. (1986) 'The Principle of Risk Classification: An Outcome Evaluation with Young Adult Probationers', *Canadian Journal of Criminology*, 28, 377–384.

Apex Scotland (2006) *Annual Report 2006* (Edinburgh: Apex Scotland).

Audit Commission (1993) *Helping with Enquiries* (London: HMSO).

_____ (1996), *Misspent Youth: Young People and Crime* (London: HMSO).

Audit Scotland (2002) *Dealing with Offending by Young People* (Edinburgh: Auditor General Accounts Commission).

Bayes, K. (1996) *Report on Freagarrach Project up to November, 1995* (unpublished).

_____ (1997) *Central Scotland Young Offenders Strategy: Review Report* (Polmont: Freagarrach Project).

Blagg, H. (1985) 'Reparation and Justice for Juveniles', *British Journal of Criminology*, 25(3), 267–279.

Boswell, G.R. (1998) 'Criminal Justice and Violent Young Offenders', *Howard Journal of Criminal Justice*, 37(2), 148–160.

Bottoms, A.E. (2002) 'The Divergent Development of Juvenile Justice Policy and Practice in England and Scotland' in *A Century of Juvenile Justice*, Rosenheim, M., Zimring, F., Tannenbaum, D. and Dohrn, B. (eds.) (Chicago: University of Chicago Press).

Braithwaite, J. (1989) *Crime, Shame and Reintegration* (Cambridge: Cambridge University Press).

_____ (1993) 'Beyond Positivism: Learning from Contextual Integrated Strategies', *Journal of Research in Crime and Delinquency*, 30(4), 383–399.

_____ (1994) 'Thinking Harder about Democratising Social Control' in *Family Conferencing and Juvenile Justice: The Way forward or Misplaced Optimism?*, Alder, C. and Wundersitz, J. (eds.) (Canberra: Australian Institute of Criminology).

_____ (1995) 'Reintegrative Shaming, Republicanism and Policy' in *Crime and Public Policy: Putting Theory to Work*, Barlow, H.D. (ed.) (Oxford: Westview Press).

_____ (1999) 'Restorative Justice: Assessing Optimistic and Pessimistic Accounts' in *Crime and Justice: A Review of Research*, Tonry, M. (ed.) (Chicago: University of Chicago Press).

Brand, S. and Price, R. (2000) *The Economic and Social Costs of Crime* (Home Office Research Study 217) (London: Home Office).

Calverley, A., Cole, B., Kaur, G., Lewis, S., Raynor, P., Sadeghi, S., Smith, D., Vanstone, M. and Wardak, A. (2004) *Black and Asian Offenders on Probation* (Home Office Research Study 277) (London: Home Office).

Campbell, B. (1993) *Goliath: Britain's Dangerous Places* (London: Methuen).

Central Regional Council, (no date) *Services for Young People in Central Region* (unpublished).

Central Scotland Police (1994) Report *of the Working Party into Juvenile Crime* (unpublished).

Central Scotland Police, Children's Reporter Administration, Barnardo's Scotland, Clackmannanshire Council, Falkirk Council and Stirling Council (1998) *Central Scotland Young Offenders Strategy June 1998* (Falkirk: Young Offenders Strategy Group).

Cleaver, H. (1991) *Vulnerable Children in Schools: A Study of Catch' Em Young* (Aldershot: Dartmouth Publishing).

Cohen, S. (1985), *Visions of Social Control* (Cambridge: Polity Press).

Collison, M. (1996) 'In Search of the High Life: Drugs, Crime, Masculinity and Consumption', *British Journal of Criminology*, 36(3), 428–444.

Coopers & Lybrand (1997) *Young People and Crime in Scotland* (Glasgow: The Prince's Trust –Action).

Crawford, A. (1997) *The Local Governance of Crime: Appeals to Community and Partnerships* (Oxford: Clarendon Press).

Denman, G. (1982) *Intensive Intermediate Treatment with Juvenile Offenders: A Handbook of Assessment and Groupwork Practice* (Lancaster: Centre of Youth, Crime and Community, Lancaster University).

Devlin, A. (1995), *Criminal Classes* (Winchester: Waterside Press).

Dodd, T. and Hunter, P. (1992) *The National Prison Survey 1991* (London: HMSO).

Doob, A.N. and Tonry, M. (2004) 'Varieties of Youth Justice' in *Youth Crime and Justice: Comparative and Cross-National Perspectives*, Tonry, M. and Doob, A.N. (eds) (Chicago: University of Chicago Press).

Downes, D. (1993) *Employment Opportunities for Offenders* (London: Home Office).

Dubourg, R., Hamed, J. and Thorns, J. (2005) *The Economic and Social Costs of Crime against Individuals and Households* (Home Office Online Report 30/05) (London: Home Office).

Farrington, D.P. (1992) 'Criminal Career Research in the United Kingdom', *British Journal of Criminology*, 32(4), 521–536.

_____ (1996), *Understanding and Preventing Youth Crime* (York: Joseph Rowntree Foundation).

_____ (1997) 'Human Development and Criminal Careers' in *The Oxford Handbook of Criminology*, Maguire, M., Morgan, R. and Reiner, R. (eds.), 2nd edn (Oxford: Oxford University Press).

Farrington, D.P., Gallagher, B., Morley, L., St Ledger, R.J. and West, D.J. (1986) 'Unemployment, School Leaving and Crime', *British Journal of Criminology*, 26(4), 335–356.

Field, S. (1990) *Trends in Crime and their Interpretation* (Home Office Research Study 119) (London: HMSO).

Freagarrach Project (1996), *Establishing Freagarrach Project* (Polmont: Freagarrach Project).

Gelsthorpe, L. (1989), *Sexism and the Female Offender* (Aldershot: Gower).

Giddens, A. (1994), *Beyond Left and Right: The Future of Radical Politics* (Cambridge: Polity Press).

Goldson, B. and Muncie, J. (eds) (2006) *Youth Crime and Justice* (London: Sage Publications).

Graham, J. and Bowling, B. (1995) *Young People and Crime* (Home Office Research Study 145) (London: Home Office).

Greenwood, P.W., Model, K.E., Rydell, C.P. and Chiesa, J. (1998) *Diverting Children from a Life of Crime: Measuring Costs and Benefits* (Santa Monica: RAND Corporation).

Hagell, A. and Newburn, T. (1994) *Persistent Young Offenders* (London: Policy Studies Institute).

Hämäläinen, J. (2003) 'The Concept of Social Pedagogy in the Field of Social Work', *Journal of Social Work*, 3(1), 69–80.

Harper, G. and Chitty, C. (2005), *The Impact of Corrections on Re-Offending: A Review of 'What Works'* (Home Office Research Study 291) (London: Home Office).

Hirschi, T. (1969) *Causes of Delinquency* (Berkeley, CA: University of California Press).

Hollin, C. (1995) 'The Meaning and Implications of "Programme Integrity"' in *What Works: Reducing Reoffending*, McGuire, J. (ed.) (Chichester: John Wiley).

Hollin, C., Palmer, E., McGuire, J., Hounsome, J., Hatcher, R., Bilby, C. and Clark, C. *Pathfinder Programmes in the Probation Service: A Retrospective Analysis* (Home Office Online Report 66/04) (London: Home Office).

Hough, M. (1996) *Drug Misuse and the Criminal Justice System* (London: Home Office).

Hurley, N. (1989) *A Need to be Counted: Employment and Training Opportunities For 16–18 Year Old Offenders, Ex-Offenders, and Young People at Risk* (Edinburgh: Apex Scotland).

Karoly, L.A., Greenwood, P.W., Everingham, S.S., Houbé, J., Kilburn, M.R., Rydell, C.P., Sanders, M. and Chiesa, J. (1998) *Investing in our Children: What We Know and Don't Know about the Costs and Benefits of Early Childhood Interventions* (Santa Monica: RAND Corporation).

Kelly, A. (1996a) *Introduction to the Scottish Children's Panel* (Winchester: Waterside Press).

_____ (1996b) *Regional Reporter to the Children's Panel, Annual Report 1995* (Glenrothes: Fife Regional Council).

King, M. (1988) *How to Make Social Crime Prevention Work: The French Experience* (London: NACRO).

Knapp, M. and Netten, A. (1997) 'The Costs and Cost Effectiveness of Community Penalties: Principles, Tools and Examples', in *Evaluating the Effectiveness of Community Penalties*, Mair, G. (ed.) (Aldershot: Avebury).

Leibrich, J. (1993) *Straight to the Point: Angles on Giving Up Crime* (Dunedin: University of Otago Press).

Lewis, J. and Gibson, F. (1977) 'The Teaching of Some Social Work Skills: Towards a Skills Laboratory', *British Journal of Social Work*, 7(2), 189–209.

Lipsey, M.W. (1995) 'What do we Learn from 400 Research Studies on the Effectiveness of Treatment with Juvenile Delinquents?' in *What Works: Reducing Reoffending*, McGuire, J. (ed.) (Chichester: John Wiley).

Lloyd, C. (1995) *To Scare Straight or Educate?* The British Experience of Day Visits to Prison for Young People (Home Office Research Study 149) (London: Home Office).

Lockyer, A. and Stone, F.H. (1998) *Juvenile Justice in Scotland: Twenty-Five Years of the Welfare Approach* (Edinburgh: T. and T. Clark).

Lucas, J., Raynor, P. and Vanstone, M. (1992) *Straight Thinking on Probation: One Year On* (Bridgend: Mid-Glamorgan Probation Service).

MacAlpine, N. and Mackenzie, J. (1973) *Gaelic-English and English-Gaelic Dictionary* (Glasgow: Gairm Publications).

Mair, G., Lloyd, C. and Hough, M. (1997) 'The Limitations of Reconviction Rates', in *Evaluating the Effectiveness of Community Penalties*, Mair, G. (ed.) (Aldershot: Avebury).

Matza, D. (1964) *Delinquency and Drift* (New York: John Wiley).

McAra, L. (2006) 'Welfare in Crisis?, Key Developments in Scottish Youth Justice' in *Comparative Youth Justice*, Muncie, J. and Goldson, B. (eds) (London: Sage Publications).

McGuire, J. (1995) 'Reviewing "What Works": Past, Present and Future' in *What Works: Reducing Reoffending*, McGuire, J. (ed.) (Chichester: John Wiley).

McIvor, G. (1990) *Sanctions for Serious or Persistent Offenders: A Review of the Literature* (Stirling: Social Work Research Centre, University of Stirling).

____ (1994) 'Social Work and Criminal Justice in Scotland: Developments in Policy and Practice', *British Journal of Social Work*, 24(4), 429–448.

McIvor, G. and Moodie, K. (2002), *Evaluation of the Matrix Project* (Stirling: Social Work Research Centre, University of Stirling).

McNeill, F. (2006) 'Community Supervision: Context and Relationships Matter' in *Youth Crime and Justice*, Goldson, B. and Muncie, J. (eds) (London: Sage Publications).

McNeill, F., Batchelor, S., Burnett, R. and Knox, J. (2005) *21st Century Social Work: Reducing Re-Offending: Key Practice Skills* (Edinburgh: Scottish Executive).

Mortimore, P., Sammons, P., Stoll, L., Lewis, D. and Ecob, R. (1988) *School Matters: The Junior Years* (Shepton Mallett: Open Books).

Nuttall, C.P. (director) (1998) *Reducing Offending: An Assessment of Research Evidence on Ways of Reducing Offending Behaviour* (Home Office Research Study 187) (London: Home Office).

Palmer, T. (1992) *The Re-Emergence of Correctional Intervention* (Newbury Park, CA: Sage Publications).

Pawson, R. and Tilley, N. (1997) *Realistic Evaluation* (London: Sage Publications).

Pearson, G., Blagg, H., Smith, D., Sampson, A. and Stubbs, P. (1992) 'Crime, Community and Conflict: The Multi-Agency Approach' in *Unravelling Criminal Justice*, Downes, D. (ed.) (Basingstoke: Macmillan).

Piacentini, L. and Walters, R. (2006) 'The Politicization of Youth Crime in Scotland and the Rise of the "Burberry Court"', *Youth Justice*, 6(1), 43–59.

Popham, F., McIvor, G., Brown, A., Eley, S., Malloch, M., Murray, C., Piacentini, L., Walters, R. and Murray, L. (2005) *Evaluation of the Hamilton Youth Court Pilot 2003-2005* (Edinburgh: Scottish Executive Social Research).

Priestley, P. and McGuire, J. (1985) *Offending Behaviour: Skills and Stratagems for Going Straight* (London: Batsford).

Priestley, P., McGuire, J., Flegg, D., Hemsley, V. and Welham, D. (1978) *Social Skills and Personal Problem-Solving: A Handbook of Methods* (London: Tavistock).

Raynor, P. and Vanstone, M. (1996) 'Reasoning and Rehabilitation in Britain: The Results of the Straight Thinking on Probation (STOP) Programme', *International Journal of Offender Therapy and Comparative Criminology*, 40(4), 272–284.

Robins, D. (1992) *Tarnished Vision: Crime and Conflict in the Inner City* (Oxford: Oxford University Press).

Rumgay, J. and Cowan, S. (1998) 'Pitfalls and Prospects in Partnerships: Probation Programmes for Substance Misusing Offenders', *Howard Journal of Criminal Justice*, 37(2), 124–136.

Rutherford, A. (1986) *Growing out of Crime* (Harmondsworth: Penguin Books).

Rutter, M., Maughan, R., Mortimore, P. and Ouston, J. (1979) *Fifteen Hundred Hours: Secondary Schools and their Effects on Children* (London: Open Books).

Sampson, R.J. and Laub, J.H. (1993) *Crime in the Making: Pathways and Turning Points through Life* (Cambridge, MA: Harvard University Press).

Scheff, T.J. (1997) *Emotions, the Social Bond, and Human Reality: Part/Whole Analysis* (Cambridge: Cambridge University Press).

Scottish Executive (2000) *It's a Criminal Waste: Stop Youth Crime Now* (Edinburgh: Scottish Executive).

_____ (2002) *Scotland's Action Programme to Reduce Youth Crime* (Edinburgh: Scottish Executive).

Scottish Home and Health Department (1964) *Report of the Committee on Children and Young Persons: Scotland* (Cmnd 2306) (The Kilbrandon Report) (Edinburgh: HMSO).

Scottish Office (1992) *The Report of the Enquiry into Child Care Policies in Fife* (The Kearney Report) (Edinburgh: Scottish Office).

_____ (1993) *Scotland's Children: Proposals for Child Care Policy and Law* (Edinburgh: HMSO).

_____ (1994) *Persistent Young Offenders: Outline Specification for Development Project* (unpublished).

_____ (1995), *Referrals of Children to Reporters and Children's Hearings 1994*, (Statistical Bulletin, Social Work Series) (Edinburgh: Scottish Office).

_____ (1998), *Costs, Sentencing Profiles and the Scottish Criminal Justice System 1996* (Edinburgh: Scottish Office).

_____ (1999) *Costs, Sentencing Profiles and the Scottish Criminal Justice System 1997* (Edinburgh: Scottish Office).

Smith, D. (1995) *Criminology for Social Work* (Basingstoke: Macmillan).

_____ (1997) *'How Much Do We Really Know about What Really Works?'*, Information: The Reality and the Potential, Proceedings of the 13th Annual Probation Information and Research Conference (Worcester, Midlands Probation Training Consortium).

_____ (2000) 'Learning from the Scottish Juvenile Justice System', *Probation Journal*, 47(1), 12–17.

_____ (2003) 'Comparative Criminal Justice: North and South of the Border', *Vista: Perspectives on Probation 6*, 2-8.

_____ (2005) 'Probation and Social Work', *British Journal of Social Work*, 35(5), 621–637.

Smith, D. and Blagg, H. (1989) 'The Cumbrian Reparation Scheme', *British Journal of Social Work*, 19(3), 255–275.

Smith, D. and Stewart, J. (1998) 'Probation and Social Exclusion' in *Crime and Social Exclusion*, Jones Finer, C. and Nellis, M. (eds) (Oxford: Blackwell Publishing).

Soothill, K. (1974) *The Prisoner's Release* (London: Allen & Unwin).

South, N. (2002) 'Drugs, Alcohol and Crime' in *The Oxford Handbook of Criminology*. Maguire, M., Morgan, R. and Reiner, R. (eds), 3rd edn (Oxford: Oxford University Press).

Stern, V. (1996) 'Let the Ex-Cons Back In', *The Guardian*, 2 May, 15.

Stewart, G. and Stewart, J. (1993), *Social Circumstances of Younger Offenders Under Supervision* (Wakefield: ACOP).

Stewart, J., Smith, D. and Stewart, G. (1994) *Understanding Offending Behaviour* (Harlow: Longman).

Sykes, G.M. and Matza, D. (1957) 'Techniques of Neutralization: A Theory of Delinquency', *American Sociological Review*, 22(6), 664–670.

Thorpe, D.H., Smith, D., Green, C.J. and Paley, J.H. (1980), *Out of Care: The Community Support of Juvenile Offenders* (London: Allen & Unwin).

Tilley, N. (1992) *Safer Cities and Community Safety Strategies* (Crime Prevention Paper 38) (London: Home Office).

_____ (1993) *After Kirkholt: Theory, Method and Results of Replication Evaluations* (Police Research Group Paper 47) (London: HMSO).

Truax, C.B. and Carkhuff, R.R. (1967) *Towards Effective Counselling and Psychotherapy* (Chicago: Aldine).

Whyte, B. (2000) 'Between Two Stools: Youth Justice in Scotland', *Probation Journal*, 47(2), 119–125.

—— (2003) 'Young and Persistent: Recent Developments in Youth Justice Policy and Practice in Scotland', *Youth Justice*, 3(2), 74–85.

Index